MOTSON'S
NATIONAL OBSESSION
The Greatest Football Trivia Book Ever...

Printed and bound in Great Britain by MPG Books Ltd, Bodmin

Distributed in the US by Publishers Group West

Arcane is an imprint of Sanctuary Publishing Limited
Sanctuary House, 45–53 Sinclair Road
London W14 0NS, United Kingdom

www.sanctuarypublishing.com

Cover: Ashley Western at Ghost Design
Illustrations: Axos

ISBN: 1-86074-601-2

MOTSON'S
NATIONAL OBSESSION

The Greatest Football Trivia Book Ever...

Adam Ward with John Motson OBE

arcane

— ACKNOWLEDGEMENTS —

Thanks to Nick Constable, Karen Farrington, Jeremy Griffin, Graham McColl, Rab MacWilliam and Ivan Ponting.

— ADAM WARD: AN APPRECIATION —

The first time I met Adam was over ten years ago when I was Publisher at Hamlyn Books and interviewing for a Sports Editor. He turned up for the interview and within just a few minutes I knew he was the man for the job. A tall, amiable young fellow, with an engaging personality and a seemingly permanent grin, he was a true football enthusiast (West Ham in his case, Arsenal in mine, but we soon overcame that potential obstacle).

Adam demonstrated a prodigious capacity for hard work, combined with an unerring eye for detail and a sharp and incisive intellect. With his ebullient nature, his constant supply of wisecracks and perceptive observations, and his ability to raise the mood of anyone around him, Adam was impossible to dislike. We quickly became friends and collaborated on a number of sports books. He was at the same time responsible and irreverent, knowing when a situation required dispassionate and serious attention but also when the only conceivable reaction was one of ironic and often hilarious bemusement.

I left the company to form my own writing/packaging business in 1996 but we kept in touch and continued to work on various projects together, meeting regularly at the Euston Flyer pub conveniently opposite the British Library (Adam didn't drink but joined in convivially with those who did). He went on to write regular articles for football magazines and websites (he was very big in Japan, apparently) and he was particularly proud when his *Official Illustrated History Of West Ham United* was published.

Adam recently moved to Stoke Newington in North London, where I live, and I was looking forward not only to renewing our professional relationship but also to re-establishing our friendship. The last contact I had with him was just a few days before his death when he needed to find a local doctor. His leg had been hurt playing football. 'Did you get your own back?' I said. 'No, he was only a kid. It was an accident,' he replied, with typical generosity. When I heard the news that he had been killed in a car crash I simply couldn't believe it. Everyone who knew Adam – and he had a wide circle of friends – felt the loss deeply.

Adam was an entertaining companion and a talented man, who unfairly and tragically died at the age of 33. I hope that this book stands as fitting memorial to his work and that his two young sons Joe and Tom will, as they grow older, appreciate the admiration and affection which their father inspired.

Rab MacWilliam
London
March 2004

— FOREWORD —

They are still there on my bookshelf, 50 years later: 20 volumes of *Charles Buchan's Soccer Gift Book*, the Christmas present I looked forward to most. Neither can I bring myself to dispose of two other favourite boyhood annuals: *The Big Book Of Football Champions* and *The Boy's Book Of Soccer*.

Yes, I grew up eventually. Then I started a collection of programmes, handbooks, club histories, and pre-season publications, like the *Rothmans Football Yearbook* (a full set I am proud to say) and the *Playfair* and *News Of The World* annuals. Obsessed? Most definitely. Little wonder I finished up as a football commentator. Looking back, my bookshelf never gave me the chance for anything else.

Not being able to resist a football quiz; always ready to commit to memory those connections and coincidences that pepper the conversation when football fans get together; happy to join in the argument over whether a certain player won an international cap or played in a Cup final: I plead guilty to all charges.

Other books in this series assure me there are plenty of other obsessives to keep me company, but for this one I have to thank Adam Ward for his discipline and dedication. Does that make him sound more like a footballer? Allow me to reveal that he is, at a modest level, even sustaining a footballing injury while in the throes of compiling this book. As you will see in the pages ahead, it did not deter him from detail.

I was prepared to be surprised by the depth of his research, and I am not disappointed. From quirky kits to Nazi salutes, and from Fatty Foulke to Arthur Wharton, you will discover bar-room banter offering an enjoyable happy-hour cocktail of history and humour.

How did Herbert Chapman manage to intoxicate his opposite number while conducting a transfer and remain sober himself? And who were the two luminaries on either side of Liverpool's Albert Stubbins on the cover of The Beatles' *Sergeant Pepper's Lonely Hearts Club Band* album?

At no point in its compilation was the script set in stone. Nothing stands still in football, and as the deadline date loomed we were still wondering whether Arsenal would go through the League season unbeaten. One title they were always going to win comes under the heading 'Cricketing Footballers', and if you support a different London club, worry not – the section on London rivalries is just for you!

I can assure you I have only scratched the surface of what lies ahead, but I promise there is a mention of *Match Of The Day* in there somewhere, and I also guarantee this *is* a book you will want to put down – only so you can pick it up again more frequently.

John Motson
Hertfordshire
March 2004

— TEN RULES THAT ARE NO MORE —

1. Kicking an opponent in the shins – Outlawed in 1863 by the fledgling FA.

2. Carrying the ball – Banned in 1863, at which point those who couldn't bear to put the ball down began playing rugby. Touching the ball was added to the list of 'don'ts' six years later.

3. One-handed throw-ins – Players told to put both hands behind the ball from 1882.

4. Offside – The offside rule was tinkered with for the first time in 1866 when it was adapted so that an attacker was onside providing three opponents were between him and the goal – previously anybody in front of the ball was offside.

5. Charging the 'keeper – Prior to 1900 it was deemed fair for a forward to charge the goalkeeper at any time. The new rule prescribed that the custodian could now only be assaulted if he had the ball in his hands.

6. Penalty area – The 18-yard box was introduced in 1901–02, superseding the old system whereby the penalty area ran across the entire width of the pitch.

7. Charging from behind – From 1904 this practice was only permitted against an opponent who was obstructing play.

8. Handling outside the penalty area (goalkeepers) – In 1910 'keepers were banned from handling the ball outside their own penalty area.

9. Obstruction – As from 1948 the offence of obstructing an opponent was punished by the award of a free-kick.

10. Substitutes – In 1965 the Football League in England permitted the use of one substitute to be used to replace an injured player. Clubs had previously been forced to play out games with reduced numbers.

— GIVE US A 'D' —

It was not until the 1937–38 season that the 'D' on the edge of the penalty area appeared on English football pitches. The arc (to give it its proper name) was added to ensure that all players were at least 10 yards (9m) away from the kicker when a penalty was taken.

— NAZI SALUTES —

When England travelled to Berlin to take on Germany in 1938 the British Ambassador insisted the players give a Nazi salute when the German national anthem was played prior to the game. The players were not entirely comfortable about the whole situation – especially since the Germans had just signalled their political intentions by marching into Austria – and captain Eddie Hapgood protested strongly. However, in the end… orders are orders, and the England team did as they were told. Thankfully the Brits made their point out on the pitch, trouncing the Germans 6–3.

— ODE TO NEVILLE —

Neville Neville, your future's immense,
Neville Neville, you play in defence,
Neville Neville, like Jacko you're bad,
Neville Neville is the name of your dad.
(to the tune of David Bowie's 'Rebel Rebel')

Sung to Gary and Phil Neville by Manchester United fans amused by the fact that their star duo's father has the same first and surnames.

— EUROPEAN FOOTBALLERS OF THE YEAR —

Nine European Footballers Of The Year have played at least part of their career in England:

		ENGLISH CLUBS	WINNING YEARS
1.	Stanley Matthews	Stoke City, Blackpool	1956
2.	Denis Law	Huddersfield Town, Manchester United, Manchester City	1964
3.	Bobby Charlton	Manchester United	1966
4.	George Best	Manchester United, Fulham, Stockport, Bournemouth	1968
5.	Allan Simonsen	Charlton Athletic	1977
6.	Kevin Keegan	Scunthorpe, Liverpool, Southampton, Newcastle United	1978 and 1979
7.	Ruud Gullit	Chelsea	1987
8.	George Weah*	Chelsea, Manchester City	1995
9.	Michael Owen	Liverpool	2001

* George Weah is also the only World Player Of The Year winner to have plied his trade in Britain.

— THE GHOST OF JOHN THOMSON —

Football fans are frequently portrayed as fickle fellows with short memories and little interest in the heroes of the past. However, at Celtic Park the tragic tale of one former player remains unforgotten. Goalkeeper John Thomson was a 22-year-old Scotland international of great promise and rising stock in 1931, but a collision with Rangers striker Sam English at Ibrox left the Celtic star with a fractured skull and within hours he was dead. No blame was attached to English, but the Rangers man was haunted by the incident and within a year he had quit Scottish football to try his luck with Liverpool. Thomson's passing remains lamented by the Celtic faithful who still remember their heroic former goalkeeper with a stirring song, the final verse of which goes as follows:

> So come all you Glasgow Celtic,
> Stand up and play the game,
> For between your posts there stands a ghost,
> Johnny Thomson is his name.

— LIVERPOOL'S GOLDEN ERA —

Bill Shankly 1959–74
First Division Champions 1963–64, 1965–66, 1972–73
FA Cup winners 1965, 1974
UEFA Cup 1973

Bob Paisley 1974–83
First Division Champions 1975–76, 1976–77, 1978–79, 1979–80, 1981–82, 1982–83
League Cup winners 1981, 1982, 1983
European Cup 1977, 1978, 1981
UEFA Cup 1976

Joe Fagan 1983–85
First Division Champions 1983–84
League Cup winners 1984
European Cup 1984

Kenny Dalglish 1985–91
First Division Champions 1985–86, 1987–88, 1989–90
FA Cup winners 1986, 1989

— MATCH OF THE DAY —

The BBC's football highlights show, *Match Of The Day*, has long been regarded as something of a national institution in England. Thursday night may have been *Top Of The Pops* and Sunday evening may (for some people) have been *Songs Of Praise*, but to football fans nationwide, Saturday evening has long been synonymous with *Match Of The Day*. The show first aired back in August 1964, with Liverpool beating Arsenal 3–2 at Anfield in the first screened game. Back then, a paying supporter could expect to gain admission to a First Division game for 5s (25p) or less.

Having lost the rights to air Premiership footage in 2001, the Beeb will be once more taking the reins for another three years, starting from the 2004–05 season.

— LONDON RIVALRIES —

The dynamic of London football is a complex thing. With 12 teams playing in the capital (13 before Wimbledon decamped to Milton Keynes in 2003), neighbours compete for bragging rights and valuable points in a stream of tense local derbies. Rivalries, of course, change over time but the current situation can be summarised as follows:

Club	Chief rivals	Also dislike	Patronising affection for
Arsenal	Tottenham	Chelsea	Leyton Orient
Brentford	QPR	Fulham	N/A
Charlton	Crystal Palace	Millwall	N/A
Chelsea	Tottenham	Arsenal	Fulham (traditionally)
Crystal Palace	Brighton*	Charlton	N/A
Fulham	Chelsea	Tottenham	N/A
Leyton Orient	West Ham	Tottenham	N/A
Millwall	West Ham	Charlton	N/A
QPR	Chelsea	Fulham	N/A
Tottenham	Arsenal	Chelsea	Leyton Orient
Watford	Luton Town*	Arsenal	N/A
West Ham	Millwall	Chelsea	Leyton Orient

* Rivalry exists despite out-of-London location

— BRIEF REIGNS —

Departed managers section – not definitive, but interesting.

Although Terry tops this list, seven games is hardly a fair crack o' the whip for anybody. Indeed, his Northampton side was receiving a pummelling either side of his tenure so, really, it's time to let this one go, Cobblers fans.

Who knows what Fenwick might have achieved given a little patience? Sunderland manager Mick McCarthy began his career at The Stadium Of Light in the style of a British Eurovision Song Contest entry. But after losing his first nine games in the Premiership at the end of the 2002–03 season, Mick admirably steadied the ship. As we go to press, Sunderland have an FA Cup semi-final place and are well in the hunt for the First Division play-offs.

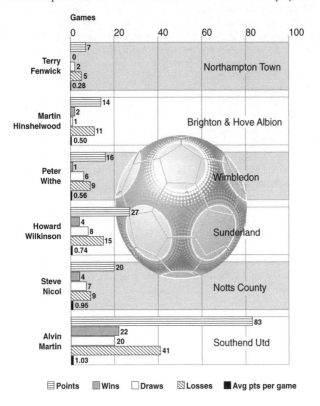

Games

	Points	Wins	Draws	Losses	Avg pts per game
Terry Fenwick — Northampton Town	7	0	2	5	0.28
Martin Hinshelwood — Brighton & Hove Albion	14	2	1	11	0.50
Peter Withe — Wimbledon	16	1	6	9	0.56
Howard Wilkinson — Sunderland	27	4	8	15	0.74
Steve Nicol — Notts County	20	4	7	9	0.95
Alvin Martin — Southend Utd	83	22	20	41	1.03

☰ Points � Wins ☐ Draws ⧅ Losses ■ Avg pts per game

— ERIC CANTONA IN BRIEF —

Born: Paris, 24 May 1966

Auxerre 1983–88

Eric makes his mark on not only French football but also his own team-mates during the characteristically explosive formative years of his career. The promising young striker nets 23 goals in 81 League appearances, chins his own 'keeper (giving him a black eye) and is handed a three-month ban for a dangerous tackle. He also finds time to make his international debut, scoring in a 2–1 defeat against West Germany.

Marseille 1988–89

L'enfant terrible makes a record-breaking £2m move to the Riviera and helps his new club to a League and Cup double. However, on the international front things aren't going quite so well. It seems describing your national team manager as a 'bag of shit' is seen as something of a *faux pas* in France. Worse follows when Eric finds himself banned indefinitely after kicking a ball into the crowd during a game.

Bordeaux 1989

The list of misdemeanours grows ever longer, and when Eric chucks his shirt at the ref after being substituted, he is on his way out of Marseille. A loan move to Bordeaux sees the 22-year-old score an impressive six goals in 11 appearances; however, absences from training bring an end to his stay at the club.

Montpellier 1989–90

Eric's transfer-market value falls to a modest £300,000 but his capacity to both score goals and shock remains spectacularly impressive. Ten goals (and a French Cup winner's medal) are accompanied by a ten-match ban after a scrap with a team-mate climaxes with Cantona throwing his boots in the face of his colleague.

Marseille 1990–91

Eric's second stint at the Vélodrome is remarkably free from major incident. There are goals, injuries and the occasional fallings out with colleagues (most notably coach Raymond Goethals), but this is merely the calm before the storm.

Nimes 1991–92
Having kept sports reporters busy for the better part of a decade, Eric says farewell to French football in typically controversial style. He throws the ball in the face of a referee, fights with an opponent and is suspended for two months. The final straw comes at a disciplinary committee meeting when Eric calls each member of the panel an 'idiot' in turn. The big-wigs at the French FA aren't impressed... but Eric doesn't really care. He decides to retire.

Leeds United 1992
Eric arrives in Britain as a relative unknown, joining Leeds United for just £900,000 after Sheffield Wednesday manager Trevor Francis dithers over signing the Frenchman. He instantly becomes a cult hero and scores nine goals to help the Elland Road side to the League Championship. Inexplicably, however, he is transferred to rivals Manchester United the following winter. Leeds fans are unimpressed.

Manchester United 1992–97
At the age of 26, Eric begins the most intriguing (and also the final) chapter of his dramatic career. In five years at United the highs unquestionably outweigh the controversial lows and by the time 'King Eric' quits the game in 1997 he has become an Old Trafford legend to rank alongside Charlton, Law and Best. The Frenchman's love affair with United begins instantly, with Eric inspiring United to their first League title for 26 years. Even greater glory follows in the shape of the League and Cup double in 1994; though a different double (two sendings off in consecutive games in mid-season) suggests that Eric is not yet free from the kind of problems that dogged his career in France. The now notorious assault on a Crystal Palace fan in 1995 leads to a lengthy ban and is unquestionably Eric's nadir in English football. With their talismanic striker absent, United fail to win the Premiership, but it is business as usual when he returns. In 1995–96 Eric is made club captain and leads the Reds to a second double, collecting the Footballer Of The Year award on route. Another Championship duly follows (the fourth in five years for United and the fifth in six for Cantona) before Eric stuns the football world by announcing his retirement from the game on Sunday 18 May 1997. He is still only 30 years old.

— RANGERS CLINCH EUROPEAN CROWN —

In 1972 Glasgow giants Rangers enjoyed arguably their greatest success, defeating Moscow Dynamo 3–2 in the European Cup Winners' Cup final. Twenty thousand jubilant Glaswegians travelled to the game in Barcelona, and many were overwhelmed by their team's breathtaking performance. The Gers swept aside their Russian opponents, surging into a 3–0 lead after 50 minutes, courtesy of goals from Colin Stein and Willie Johnston (2). However, such was the charged atmosphere that each Rangers goal was succeeded by a pitch invasion.

The interruptions fractured the Scots' rhythm and Dynamo came back into the game, scoring twice to leave the previously animated Gers fans chewing their nails and praying for the final whistle. The referee duly obliged and after a collective intake of breath, the fans in royal blue once more invaded the pitch. This time the Spanish police greeted them with a baton charge and a full-scale pitch battle resulted. One man died and more than 150 were injured.

The inevitable fallout from the post-match *mêlée* saw Rangers banned from European competition for a year. However, they could still count themselves lucky, as Dynamo had been angling to have the game replayed. As a postscript to the whole saga, goalscorers Johnston and Stein were both sold at the start of the following season, while manager Willie Waddell handed the reins to Jock Wallace and took a job 'upstairs'.

— NOT LIKE WATCHING BRAZIL —

When England lost to Poland in a World Cup qualifier in June 1973 they wore yellow shirts and blue shorts. The Brazilian influence clearly did not extend beyond the sartorial.

— HEADLESS DANE PLAYS BALL —

According to legend, football was first practised in England by Anglo-Saxon warriors who celebrated victory over a Danish king by severing their enemy's head and kicking it around town.

— SVEN ON ENGLAND (PART 1) —

'I admire the English mentality because you are strong, so hard working. But we have talent.'

Future England manager Sven-Goran Eriksson offers his opinion on English football after watching his Benfica team knock Arsenal out of the European Cup in 1991.

— THE DONS LEAD THE WAY —

Aberdeen's Pittodrie Stadium was the first ground in Britain to feature a dugout, an innovation that was introduced in the 1920s at the insistence of trainer Donald Colman, who believed that he could learn much more about his players through making notes on their footwork at ground level. He required dry conditions in which to write his notes and so the club installed a dugout from which he could operate. Pittodrie also, in 1978, became the first British football ground to become all-seater, a move in which Aberdeen were followed swiftly by Clydebank.

— TOTTENHAM ODD SHIRTS —

When Tottenham Hotspur played Coventry City in the 1987 FA Cup final, several of the Spurs players wore shirts that did not display their sponsor's 'Holsten' logo. Spurs lost 3–2, with skipper Gary Mabbutt scoring a decisive own goal in extra time. Mabbutt's shirt, no doubt to the relief of Holsten, was one of the shirts free from advertising.

— CRICKETING FOOTBALLERS —

Ten professional footballers who also played first-class cricket:

Ian Botham	(Scunthorpe and Somerset)
Brian Close	(Bradford City and Yorkshire)
Denis Compton*	(Arsenal and Middlesex)
Les Compton	(Arsenal and Middlesex)
Bill Edrich	(Tottenham and Middlesex)
Geoff Hurst	(West Ham and Essex)
Arthur Milton*	(Arsenal and Gloucestershire)
Phil Neale	(Lincoln City and Worcestershire)
Jim Standen	(West Ham and Worcestershire)
Ken Taylor	(Huddersfield Town and Yorkshire)

* Also represented England at both cricket and football.

— USA SINK ENGLAND —

England, along with hosts Brazil, were favourites for the 1950 World Cup finals. The USA, who had no professional league to draw upon and whose star player was a Scotsman who had been released by Third Division Wrexham, were most certainly not among the pre-tournament favourites. When the two teams met on a bumpy pitch in Belo Horizonte, England were expected to enjoy something akin to shooting practice. An easy victory was apparently assured. However, things did not run to plan. The Americans had not read the script and scored the game's only goal when Joe Gaetjens headed in their only chance. The English quickly began to complain... the crowd were too close, the pitch was too hard, they were still tired from a long season. But the excuses could not disguise the fact that they had lost in humiliating fashion to a team of part-timers from a country which was largely uninterested in soccer.

— GREAT RESULT —

When Forfar played East Fife in the old Scottish Second Division during the 1963–64 campaign the final score was... wait for it...

Forfar 5, East Fife 4

— A BOOT FIT FOR A KING —

The classic Puma King football boot was famously worn by Eusebio in the 1966 World Cup finals, at which he ended the tournament as Golden Boot winner. It remains a best-seller to this day. Ryan Giggs, Stuart Pearce and Paul Gascoigne are among the long list of top players who have worn Puma Kings at some point during their career.

— HERBERT CHAPMAN DIES —

Herbert Chapman was undoubtedly the most successful club manager of the inter-war years and arguably the greatest Arsenal boss of all time. Chapman built a Gunners team that would claim five League Championships in the 1930s, but on 6 January 1934 the affable Yorkshireman died unexpectedly. The Arsenal manager had caught a heavy cold while on scouting missions in Bury and Sheffield, and, ignoring doctors' advice to stay at home and rest, instead went to watch Arsenal's third team on a bitterly cold day in Guildford. Chapman's cold turned into pneumonia, and 36 hours later he was dead.

Within hours, Arsenal's players were arriving at Highbury for a vital match against Sheffield Wednesday. Winger Cliff Bastin later recalled: 'As I approached the ground, the newspaper sellers were shouting out the news of Chapman's death. It seemed just too bad to be true. In the dressing room nobody had anything to say, yet each of us knew what [the others] were thinking. Herbert had been loved by us all.'

George Allison took over as Arsenal manager and completed the job that Chapman had started, leading the team to back-to-back Championships in 1933–34 and 1934–35 and the FA Cup in 1936.

— FRENCH THREAT LEADS TO BRITISH BAN —

The playing of football was banned during the reigns of Edward III, Richard II and Henry IV. All three monarchs were concerned about the threat posed by France (just as Sven-Goran Eriksson is ahead of Euro 2004) and it was felt football was an unwelcome distraction from the pursuit of archery.

— FRANK ADMIRATION —

Frank Swift is rightly regarded as one of the greatest goalkeepers in English football history. Swift enjoyed a glorious career with Manchester City, playing more than 350 times for the Blues and winning both League and Cup honours, along with 19 England caps. However, success did not always sit easily with Frank, and when he enjoyed his first brush with glory as an FA Cup winner at Wembley in 1934, the tall Lancastrian fainted after the match as a result of 'nervous strain'. Thankfully, Frank soon learned to deal with success and adulation. Frank was sadly among those who died in the Munich air disaster of 1958 – he had been travelling with the Manchester United team as a journalist.

— FIVE PENALTIES IN HALF AN HOUR —

When Crystal Palace took on Brighton in a Second Division game in March 1989, referee Kelvin Morton made history by awarding five penalties in the space of just 27 minutes. The penalties ran as follows:

Palace are 1–0 up, Brighton are down to ten men and Mark Bright scores to make it 2–0.

Minutes later Palace win another spot-kick, but this time Bright sees his effort saved by 'keeper John Keeley.

Palace win a third penalty in five minutes. Bright passes responsibility to Ian Wright, who misses.

After a ten-minute period either side of half time without incident, Morton breaks the monotony by awarding another penalty. This time he gives it to Brighton, who score courtesy of Alan Curbishley. The score is now 2–1 to Palace.

The fifth and final penalty goes to Palace, who miss again, this time through John Pemberton.

The game ended 2–1 to Crystal Palace.

— STRIKING THE RIGHT NOTE —

The father of American jazz legend Gil Scott-Heron was a Jamaican professional footballer who played for Celtic in the 1950s. Gilbert, who was nicknamed the 'Black Arrow', scored on his debut against Morton in 1951–52 but lasted barely a year at Parkhead before departing for spells with Third Lanark and Kidderminster Harriers.

— STUBBINS ON THE COVER —

Liverpool striker Albert Stubbins appears on the cover of The Beatles' *Sergeant Pepper's Lonely Hearts Club Band* album. For the record (no pun intended), he stands between George Bernard Shaw and Sri Lahiri Mahasaya.

— OLYMPIC NET HISTORIC WIN FOR NORTH —

The first northern team to win the FA Cup was Blackburn Olympic who defeated the holders Old Etonians 2–1 at Kennington Oval in 1883. The Olympic team was made up of working men who combined their football careers with various trades, and their XI included a plumber, a spinner, a metal worker and two weavers. Old Etonians, of course, were 'gentlemen players' from the south.

Olympic's victory was followed by a trio of successes for neighbours Blackburn Rovers. English football's balance of power had swung north and it was not until Tottenham Hotspur won the Cup in 1901 that a club from the south clinched a major trophy.

— MODERN FOOTBALL IS BORN —

The Football Association was born on 26 October 1863 in the Freemasons' Tavern on Great Queen Street, London, and was the brainchild of Old Harrovian Charles Alcock. The Association's primary aim was to formalise and unify the rules of a sport which had previously varied wildly from region to region.

CELEBRITY FOOTBALLERS' WIVES — AND GIRLFRIENDS (AND EXES) —

Victoria Beckham (singer) – **David Beckham**
Sheree Murphy (actress) – **Harry Kewell**
Joy Beverley (singer) – **Billy Wright**
Ulrika Jonsson (TV presenter) – **Stan Collymore**
Louise Redknapp (singer) – **Jamie Redknapp**
Davina Taylor (actress) – **Ryan Giggs**
Michelle Gayle (actress/singer) – **Mark Bright**
Leslie Ash (actress) – **Lee Chapman**
Dani Behr (TV presenter) – **Les Ferdinand**
Miss Worlds (several) – **George Best**

— FROM BRIGADE TO NATIONAL SERVICE —

Former England striker Paul Goddard was once a Warrant Officer in the Boys' Brigade. Paul's association with the Brigade earned him the nickname 'Sarge' during his time with QPR, West Ham and Newcastle.

— THE YEAR OF THE FOX —

Mascots are big business in the modern world of football. At some clubs, the mascot gets more fan mail than many of the players. They have agents, they give interviews and make public appearances. Not bad for a man – or woman – dressed up in a fluffy suit and a pair of comedy football boots. The highlight of the mascot calendar is undoubtedly the annual Mascot Grand National (MGN), which takes place at Huntingdon racecourse each September.

The 2001 MGN undoubtedly put the event on the map, and it will forever be remembered as the Year of the Fox. Or, to be more precise, the Year of Freddie Fox. Freddie's performance brought a wave of controversy and publicity that shook the mascot world to its fluffy core. But we should not mock; this was a serious business involving betting scandals, false identity and a large helping of skulduggery.

So what was it that Freddie did? Well, to start with he won the race comfortably, romping home ahead of Dazzler The Lion, mascot of Rushden And Diamonds Football Club. Officials, however, began to get suspicious when they saw that Freddie was wearing running spikes as opposed to the usual *de rigueur* large comedy boots. Freddie also aroused suspicions with vague answers to questions about his own identity and the organisation he claimed to represent, the Countryside Appreciation Group.

A stewards' enquiry was launched, with many disgruntled punters and bookmakers crying foul. A spokesman for Sportingodds, one of the firms betting on the event, said, 'We didn't feel the race was fair to punters and we are paying out on the runner-up, Dazzler The Lion, as well as the winner.' Many bookies, however, had been unwilling to get involved with the event at all, having been stung the previous year when Harry The Hornet had won after being backed from 25–1 to 3–1. Freddie's odds had followed a similar pattern – falling from 33–1 to 10–1. The suggestion was that there had been a betting coup.

Freddie was eventually unmasked and the whiff of scandal took on a decidedly noxious stench when it was revealed that the man behind the fox suit was British international hurdler Matt Douglas. He was subsequently disqualified at the request of those who entered him. Freddie's team apologised for 'spoiling' the event, and promised to donate £500 to charity, while bookmakers who took money on the winner did the same.

Meanwhile, Douglas felt that his participation had enhanced rather than spoiled the event. He said: 'I've nothing to be embarrassed about. I was running to raise money for charity, and it's put the event on the map.' He also denied any knowledge of a betting coup, despite unsubstantiated claims of involvement from a professional London-based punter.

Final word goes to Freddie himself – or rather Matt Douglas: 'An acquaintance of mine asked me in August if I would like to do a charitable event at the end of the athletics season... I was surprised when I had to run in a fox's outfit and, to be honest, I don't know anything about the Countryside Appreciation Group which I was representing.'

— THE COCKEREL THAT CROWED TOO EARLY —

In March 1987 the traditional rivalry between Arsenal and Tottenham reached new levels of intensity when the two clubs clashed in a two-legged League Cup semi-final. After seven trophyless years, Arsenal were playing with a renewed vigour under new manager George Graham, and the club was desperate to add some silverware to the centenary-season celebrations that were by now underway.

Tottenham, however, were also playing well, and in Clive Allen they had English football's most prolific marksman. True to form, Allen scored the only goal of the first leg at Highbury, and when he struck again in the return at White Hart Lane, Tottenham's fans could not contain their glee. At half time, Spurs clearly believed they were heading for the final, and with that in mind they somewhat presumptuously began to announce details of ticketing arrangements for the Wembley showpiece.

The Cockerels of Spurs had crowed too early, and goals from Viv Anderson and Niall Quinn put Arsenal back on terms and earned a replay. The flick of a coin determined that the final instalment of this trilogy would be played out at White Hart Lane. Allen again opened the scoring, but despite his three goals he finished on the losing side. A goal from Ian Allinson drew the scores level and then in the dying moments of the game, David Rocastle struck the winner. It was the first time that Arsenal had taken the lead in the 300 minutes of this epic encounter. In the final, against Liverpool, Arsenal again came from behind to win 2–1.

— CORACLE MAN —

Occasional giant-killer Shrewsbury Town FC is the only club in English football history to have had a 'coracle paddler' on the payroll. For readers who struggle with seafaring terminology, a coracle is a small, round boat traditionally made from woven willow shoots. Shrewsbury's coracle man came into his own from 1910 onwards when the club moved to its Gay Meadow ground alongside the River Severn. He'd be called into action every time a Town hoofer booted the ball over the Riverside Terrace and into the drink. Cruel-tongued fans recall that sometimes he launched so many times he got seasick.

— ARSENAL'S CONTROVERSIAL 'PROMOTION' —

When competitive football resumed after the First World War, the Football League decided to expand the First Division from 20 to 22 clubs, and both Arsenal and Tottenham were among the clubs who applied for one of the extra places. Spurs, who had finished the final pre-war season in 20th place in the old First Division, appeared to have a good case for re-election. However, the Gunners had ended as the fifth-placed team in the Second Division and appeared to have no logical case for a place in the expanded top flight.

Arsenal's charismatic chairman, Sir Henry Norris, had little to work with, but campaigned ingeniously for eight months prior to the vital AGM in June 1919, as he sought to canvass support from various influential friends.

'His influence was enormous,' commented Arsenal manager Leslie Knighton on his chairman's technique. '[He would] speak to an important person there, suggesting a favour, remind a certain financier who was interested that he had once done him a good turn and been promised something in return.' This uncompromising approach proved successful, and at the vital AGM Arsenal were awarded a place in the First Division while Tottenham were not. It had, no doubt, helped Norris's case that he was close friends with League president John McKenna, who ensured the motion was passed without the need for a vote.

— CELEBRITY SUPPORTERS —

Jo Brand – Crystal Palace
Ray Winstone – West Ham United
Jeremy Beadle – Arsenal
John Peel – Liverpool
Damon Albarn – Chelsea
Jimmy Nail – Newcastle United
Chris Moyles – Leeds United
Alistair McGowan – Coventry City
Irvine Welsh – Hibernian
Mick Hucknall – Manchester United

— DON'T MENTION THE WAR —

'Hitler didn't tell us when he was going to send over those Doodlebugs, did he?'

England manager Bobby Robson explains why he wouldn't be announcing his team to the press ahead of a World Cup qualifier against Sweden in 1989.

— 'MY GIN AND TONIC SHALL CONTAIN NO GIN' —

When Herbert Chapman decided to strengthen his Arsenal team in 1928 he was in no mood to settle for second best, and immediately set his sights on signing Bolton's England international inside-forward, David Jack. The tall, skilful inside-right had scored the first goal in a Wembley FA Cup final when Wanderers had beaten West Ham United 2–0 in 1923 and he had also scored the only goal of the final against Manchester City three years later. The Lancashire side were reluctant to sell their best player, but a persistent Chapman eventually got Wanderers to name their price for Jack. A staggering £13,000 – almost twice the transfer record.

Bolton were almost certainly trying to deter Chapman from pursuing his interest in Jack, but the tactic was unsuccessful. The Arsenal manager arranged a meeting with the Bolton chairman and secretary at a hotel to finalise a fee. Chapman, who arrived early with his assistant Bob Wall, is said to have instructed a waiter to serve the Bolton party with double measures while ensuring that his own 'gin and tonic' contained no gin. At the end of the evening, a fee of £11,500 had been agreed for the purchase of Jack.

Despite negotiating a £1,500 discount on Bolton's original fee, the transfer of David Jack still represented a British record, and FA president Charles Clegg claimed that 'no player in the world is worth £10,000'. Fortunately, for both Chapman and Arsenal, Jack would prove his worth to the Gunners by scoring 124 goals in 208 games for the club before taking charge as manager of Southend in 1933. He had also helped Arsenal win their first silverware in the shape of the 1930 FA Cup and had starred in two Championship-winning teams.

— RECORD-BREAKING SKIPPERS —

England's longest serving captains are jointly Billy Wright and Bobby Moore, who each skippered the country's national team on 90 occasions. Wright led England in three World Cup tournaments (1950, 1954, 1958) but could not match the success of his eventual successor who skippered the team to glory at Wembley in 1966. Moore, whose reign also took in the 1970 tournament, won 57 games as skipper to Wright's 49.

— USEFUL FOOTBALL PHRASES —

Back door – Call for a team-mate to pass the ball behind him (ie via a backheel).

Feet – Call for a pass to be played into feet rather than into space.

Give and go (one-two) – An appeal for a pass on the understanding that the ball will be returned forthwith.

Hold it – This call is made by a player as he passes the ball to a team-mate (usually a centre-forward). The player receiving the ball must now try to resist the attention of any markers and hold up play until reinforcements arrive. Most strikers ignore this call (as it usually involves receiving repeated kicks to the ankles).

Leave it – Fights and altercations always begin with one player telling his team-mate to 'leave it' or 'walk away'. This call for peace is universally employed but rarely heeded.

One more – Call made by a player to a team-mate standing between him and a ball which is moving in his direction. The intermediary player should either step over the ball and let it continue its path unfettered or, alternatively, help it along its way.

Out – Shouted by defenders when they've cleared an attack and are trying to move the remaining opponents up-field.

Pick up – Find an opponent to mark and stand goal-side of him.

Square ball – A request for a sideways pass from a team-mate.

Stand up – A call usually made by a coach or manager to a defending player, warning him not to commit himself to a tackle, but instead to stay on his feet and shepherd the attacker away from danger.

— FROM THE VALLEY TO THE COSMOS —

The only player to have scored 100 League goals in both England and Italy is a South African. Eddie Firmani, who enjoyed three spells with Charlton in the 1950s and 1960s, also plied his trade for both Sampdoria and Inter Milan. Eddie went on to enjoy success as a manager in America, first with Tampa and later with New York Cosmos.

— ARTHUR WHARTON —

Britain's first black footballer was goalkeeper Arthur Wharton who stood between the posts for both Rotherham and Sheffield United during the 1890s. Arthur, who ended his career with Stockport County in 1901, made 41 League appearances and is said to have been an agile and brave goalkeeper.

— CLEMENCE LEAVES SKEGGY BEHIND —

In the summer of 1967 Ray Clemence, the then teenage Scunthorpe goalkeeper, was also employed as a deckchair attendant on Skegness beach. No first-class trips to the Maldives, nor hedonistic holidays in the Balearics to illuminate this young 'keeper's first summer as a pro! An off-season wage of £9 would barely stretch to a fortnight's B&B in Scarborough. A part-time job was called for, and so it was that young Ray roamed the prom at Skeggy, checking for freeloaders while passing out stripy canvas seating to the resort's well-heeled beachgoers. Fortunately for Ray, his deckchair days were brought to a sudden and surprising end when his family forwarded him a telegram that called for him to report back to Scunthorpe FC at his earliest convenience. A move to Liverpool beckoned, and 24 hours later Bill Shankly had got his man for a fee of £18,000. For the record, Ray returned to deckchair duty for the remainder of the summer. He would, of course, go on to see rather more esteemed service with Liverpool, Tottenham Hotspur and England, with whom he won 61 senior caps.

— BROTHERLY LOVE —

Ronald and Frank De Boer, who both played for Rangers in the 2003–04 season, are not the only brothers who have played alongside each other throughout their careers. The De Boer siblings began at Ajax before transferring to Barcelona and then on to Ibrox where they were reunited after a short spell apart (Frank had detoured via Galatasaray on his way to Glasgow). However, the Dutch duo's record pales into insignificance when compared to that of Scotsmen Frank and Hugh O'Donnell who played for... wait for it... St Agatha School, Leven, Fifeshire, Denbeath Violet, Wellesley Juniors Celtic, Preston, Blackpool, Hearts and Liverpool during the 1940s and 1950s. Their parents must have been so proud.

— OTHER BROTHERS —

And, just for the record, here are ten other sets of brothers who have played for the same club:

Ian and David Brightwell (Manchester City)
Denis and Les Compton (Arsenal)
Eddie and Frank Gray (Leeds United)
Jimmy and Brian Greenhoff (Manchester United and Rochdale)
Bob and David Latchford (Birmingham City)
Gary and Phil Neville (Manchester United)
Neil and Bruce Rioch (Aston Villa)
Ian and Glynn Snodin (Doncaster Rovers)
Danny, Rod and Ray Wallace (Southampton – Rod and Ray
also played together at Leeds)
Graham and Ray Wilkins (Chelsea)

— THE LEGEND OF FATTY FOULKE —

Victorians didn't really know much of political correctness; back in those good old days when toilets were outside, poverty was rife and life expectancy short there was no time for liberal sensitivities. Irishmen were all called Paddy, Scots were Jocks and if you were fat, your nickname was invariably 'Fatty'. Football is not, of course, noted for its imaginative use of nicknames, so when Dawley-born William Foulke made a name for himself with Sheffield United at the turn of the century, the 'well-built' goalkeeper was soon dubbed 'Fatty Foulke'. The moniker stuck and the 'keeper who twice won Cup finals with the Blades (1899 and 1902) quickly became one of the most celebrated characters in English football. He was 22 stones (140kg) when he hung up his boots (though bending down to undo them can't have been easy) after a spell with Chelsea.

— SOCCER ETYMOLOGY —

The word soccer came into use in the late 19th century and has its origins in the word 'As-*soc*-iation' (as in association football). The practice of adapting words in this way (and adding an '–er' ending to them) also spawned the word 'rugger' and was particularly common among young Victorian gentlemen of the time. England international C Wreford-Brown, who played for both Oxford University and Corinthians, is the man widely credited with first using the term. Americans are, of course, eternally grateful to Mr Wreford-Brown.

— SIR ALEX BACKS BRAZIL —

Sir Alex Ferguson is a man with an eye for a champion, as he proved with some astute punting on the 2002 World Cup. The Old Trafford boss was among those who backed Brazil to lift football's greatest prize in Japan and Korea at odds of 8–1.

— YOUTHFUL PROMISE —

Rocketing transfer fees, exorbitant wages and obstreperous agents have all conspired to make buying and selling footballers a tricky business. Unsurprisingly, the 1990s saw top clubs place greater emphasis on their youth set-ups and upon developing their own talent. Several clubs enjoyed particular success. For pure glory, nobody can rival Manchester United's graduates who have brought silverware to Old Trafford with staggering regularity. However, few youth coaches can be as popular with their chairman as West Ham's Tony Carr, whose prodigies have netted the Hammers more than £50m in the last five years.

Liverpool (guru – Steve Heighway)
Graduates: Robbie Fowler, Steve McManaman, Michael Owen, Jamie Carragher and Steven Gerrard.

Manchester United (gurus – Brian Kidd and Eric Harrison)
Graduates: Ryan Giggs, Gary Neville, Phil Neville, Paul Scholes, Nicky Butt and David Beckham.

Leeds United (guru – Paul Hart)
Alan Smith, Harry Kewell, Jonathan Woodgate, Paul Robinson, Ian Harte and Stephen McPhail.

West Ham United (guru – Tony Carr)
Rio Ferdinand, Frank Lampard, Joe Cole, Michael Carrick, Jermain Defoe and Glen Johnson.

— AWAY FAN QUOTAS —

It is a requirement of all Football League clubs to make provision for at least 2,000 visiting supporters at every home match. If, however, a club's capacity is less than 20,000, it may accommodate fewer visitors but must still set aside at least 10 per cent of its certified capacity.

— GOODISON BALL PLEA —

Everton are another club who have benefited greatly from developing local talent, with Francis Jeffers, Tony Hibbert and Michael Ball all graduating from the Toffeemen's academy in recent years. However, the latest and most celebrated Everton prodigy is not quite so popular with some of the club's administrative staff. Wayne Rooney may be the current darling of the sporting press but his habit of kicking a match ball into the crowd ahead of each home game has upset the bean-counters at Goodison, who reckon they're about £3,500 down on account of Wayne's pre-match generosity.

The fans have a tendency to keep the balls 'Roonaldo' sends their way, regarding them as souvenirs, and a club spokesmen told the press, 'Obviously Rooney is a world-class player and we totally understand why fans want the balls as souvenirs. But they are not cheap items and we would ask the fans to remember the club's finances as well. We would urge all supporters to throw the balls back onto the pitch.'

— THEY USED TO WEAR... —

Arsenal ....Red and blue stripes (1890s)
Bolton Wanderers ....White with red spots (1884–85)
Coventry City...Black shirts (1880s)
Everton ....Salmon pink shirts (1890s)
Leeds United ....Blue shirts with yellow trim (1959–63)
Liverpool..Blue and white halves (1890s)
Newcastle United............................Red and white stripes (1890s)
Watford.......................Red, yellow and green hoops (1900–1909)
West Bromwich Albion ....Yellow and white quarters (1881–82)
York City...................................Yellow and brown stripes (1930s)

— REF PAYS HIGH PRICE FOR ORDER —

'Never mix work and pleasure' was the costly lesson learned by one amateur referee who found himself out of a job after booking his boss and a colleague for swearing at him during a match in 2003. The ref, who reported both men to the FA for swearing at him, claimed he was ignored and even attacked by a colleague when he returned to work. Shortly afterwards he was laid off.

— OLD FIRM TIMELINE —

1873

Rangers formed by a group of young men from the Gare Loch who had been part of the same rowing club. Initially they play on Glasgow Green but soon move to the south side of Glasgow.

1888

Celtic formed in the East End of Glasgow after Brother Walfrid, a Marist brother, has the idea of creating a football club to raise funds to feed the poor. Celtic's inaugural match in May 1888, watched by 2,000 spectators, is a 5–2 friendly victory over Rangers. Afterwards players and officials of both clubs retire for a sing-song and refreshments.

1899

They meet in the Scottish Cup final for the first time, Celtic triumphing 2–0.

1904

'Old Firm' nickname is applied jointly to the clubs before the Scottish Cup final, which Celtic win 3–2. The nickname will stick to the two clubs for the next century (see page 91).

1909

A replayed Old Firm Scottish Cup final ends in a riot at Hampden Park that rages for hours – but with supporters joining together in rage at the authorities, rather than antagonising each other. Fans of both sides had expected extra time after a 1–1 draw and when it did not materialise they suspected the officials of both sides had conspired with the Scottish Football Association to end the replay after 90 minutes in order to obtain the prospective gate receipts from a third match. No third match is played, both clubs are fined heavily, and the Cup is subsequently withheld by the SFA for the only time in Scottish Cup history.

1925

Celtic beat Rangers 5–0 in a Scottish Cup semi-final played in front of 102,000 at Hampden, the first six-figure attendance for a Scottish club match.

1928

Rangers win the Scottish Cup final 4–0, but the 1920s have seen Old Firm encounters disfigured by sectarianism, scarring the rivalry between the two clubs. Celtic are identified as the team associated with Catholics and Rangers with Protestants.

1931
Celtic goalkeeper John Thomson dies after sustaining a depressed fracture of the skull in an accidental collision with Rangers' Sam English during an Old Firm match at Ibrox.

1938
Rangers are the visitors as a record attendance of 92,000 at Celtic Park on 1 January sees Celtic win the traditional New Year's Day Old Firm fixture 3–0.

1939
Celtic return the favour of the previous year by helping to draw a record 118,500 crowd to Ibrox for the match with Rangers on 2 January. Rangers win 2–1.

1945
A crowd of more than 40,000 at Ibrox sees Rangers win 5–3 in the first post-war League match between the Old Firm sides.

1957
Celtic defeat Rangers 7–1 in the League Cup final – the record winning scoreline in a British cup final.

1963
The Old Firm Scottish Cup final and its replay attract a combined attendance of 250,000 at Hampden Park. Rangers win the second match emphatically, by 3–0, with Celtic supporters melting off the terraces long before the end.

1967
A 2–2 draw at Ibrox in a League match in May allows Celtic to secure their first treble of League Cup, Scottish Cup and League title.

1969
Jock Stein's Celtic sweep Rangers aside in the Scottish Cup final by 4–0 to seal their second treble in three years.

1971
Sixty-six fans die and many more are injured after the Old Firm League match at Ibrox on 2 January after a crush of bodies on a stairway leading from the terraces to the exit. It is, at the time, Britain's worst football disaster.

— OLD FIRM TIMELINE (CONT'D) —

1973

The last crowd of 100,000-plus to watch a club match in Scotland, an attendance of 122,714, witnesses the Old Firm contest the centenary Scottish Cup final. Rangers win 3–2.

1977

Alfie Conn, a Rangers star of the early 1970s and one of their scorers in the 1973 Cup final, returns to Scotland from Tottenham Hotspur to join Celtic and become the first post-war player to represent both sides of the Old Firm.

1980

An Old Firm Scottish Cup final, won 1–0 by Celtic, ends with a riot on the pitch after the final whistle, which is broken up by mounted police with batons drawn. As a consequence, alcohol is subsequently banned from the terraces of Scottish football grounds.

1987

A fracas in a 2–2 draw at Ibrox sees Frank McAvennie of Celtic and Terry Butcher and Chris Woods of Rangers dismissed. All three, plus Rangers' Graham Roberts, are summoned to appear in court where Woods and Butcher are convicted and fined.

1989

Rangers manager Graeme Souness signs ex-Celtic striker Maurice Johnston to make him the first Catholic-born player to represent Rangers in the modern era. Johnston had weeks earlier appeared at a press conference at Celtic Park to pledge his return to Celtic from Nantes, but had subsequently stalled on the move, allowing Souness to swoop.

1999

Rangers, fielding a team now featuring several Catholics, obtain a 3–0 victory over Celtic that sees them clinch the Scottish League title at Celtic Park for the first time. Two Celtic players are sent off and disturbances break out in and around the ground. One Celtic supporter falls from the top tier of the stand but survives, and referee Hugh Dallas is struck by coins thrown from the terraces.

2003

Rangers win a record 50th League title on the final day of the season. Both Celtic and Rangers end the season jointly on 97 points, but Rangers, having scored one more goal than Celtic, take the title on goal difference.

— CRUCIATE LIGAMENTS —

These days, no self-respecting supporter can afford to be without an intimate working knowledge of the cruciate ligament. Just like the new offside interpretation, it's vital to be able to bluff your way through terrace conversations that begin along the lines of, 'They reckon Big Dave's done a crewshit, then...' Gazza and Alan Shearer are two of the biggest names to have suffered this injury.

There are two cruciate ligaments – the posterior and the anterior – which cross over in the middle to stop your knee sliding backwards and forwards. The medial collateral and lateral collateral ligaments stop the joint wobbling from side to side. Cruciates tend to get damaged by twisting movements or a high tackle to the side of the knee. For professionals, surgery is usually the best option.

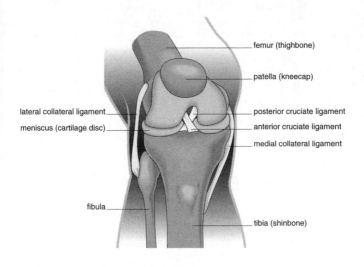

— FORTY-FOUR DAYS —

Brian Clough's ill-fated reign as Leeds United manager in 1974 lasted for just 44 days, the same length of time as American illusionist David Blaine spent in a perspex box suspended over the River Thames in 2003.

— HALL OF FAME INDUCTEES —

In 2002 the National Football Museum in Preston inaugurated its hall of fame by honouring 29 people who were considered to have made an 'outstanding and lasting contribution to English football'. The inductees were chosen by a panel of 20 football luminaries which included Sir Bobby Charlton, Sir Alex Ferguson, Sir Bobby Robson, Terry Venables, Mark Lawrenson and Brian Clough. The 29 were:

Players:
Gordon Banks
George Best
Eric Cantona
John Charles
Bobby Charlton
Kenny Dalglish
Dixie Dean
Peter Doherty
Duncan Edwards
Tom Finney
Paul Gascoigne
Jimmy Greaves
Johnny Haynes
Kevin Keegan
Denis Law
Nat Lofthouse
Dave Mackay

Players (cont'd):
Stanley Matthews
Bobby Moore
Bryan Robson
Peter Shilton
Billy Wright

Managers:
Matt Busby
Brian Clough
Alex Ferguson
Bob Paisley
Alf Ramsey
Bill Shankly

Female Player:
Lily Parr

— KEEGAN... THE NEW HADRIAN —

Kevin Keegan recently revealed that he likes to build brick walls in his spare time. The former European Footballer Of The Year has turned his back on traditional extra-curricular activities like golf and horse racing, and has instead developed a keen interest in construction. He told the Manchester City website, 'I love building brick walls when I am out of the game. My wife calls me Hadrian, as I have this habit of building walls when I have time on my hands.'

However, Keegan was quick to refute the suggestion that he would be trading his tracksuit for work boots and a white van any day soon: 'The game is in your blood... there is only so much gardening and decorating you can do.'

— COPA MUNDIAL PROVES A CHAMPION —

The best-selling football boot in the world
is reputed to be the Adidas Copa Mundial,
which was first produced in 1979 and
designed specifically for the 1982 FIFA
World Cup in Spain.

— GIGGS: 100 PER CENT WELSH —

Throughout his career Ryan Giggs has been criticised, albeit via a whispering
campaign, for choosing to play for Wales rather than England. The argument
is based on the assumption that because Giggs played for England Schoolboys
he should have continued to wear the white shirt rather than the red that he
took up at Youth International level. However, the player, who was born in
Cardiff to Welsh parents, refutes this suggestion and is incensed by its
implications:

'The problem came because I played for England Schoolboys. But that was
because I went to school in England, no other reason; that was the criteria
for selection, not where you were born. What has bugged me more than
anything in my career is to keep on hearing people say I chose to play for
Wales. I still hear it, people discussing it on the radio even now. It's very,
very annoying for me. It's the question that has bugged me most for the last
10 years or so.

'I am Welsh, 100 per cent. End of story. Both my parents and all my
grandparents are Welsh. It's as simple as that... it's impossible for me to play
for England.'

— KNOW MY NAME —

Back in the spring of 1988 George Graham was putting the finishing
touches to an Arsenal team that would soon be champions and which
was rapidly earning a reputation for its curmudgeonly and unyielding
defensive play. But when the Gunners took on Southampton towards
the end of that 1987–88 season, their usually thrifty defence was undone
by a rookie striker who had quietly risen through the Saints' youth
ranks. Southampton's new frontman struck three times in a 4–2 victory
to become the youngest player to score a hat-trick in a First Division
game. He was just 17 years and 140 days old. His name? Alan Shearer.

— FROM POISON PEN TO THE DEN —

'I always answer letters from supporters; it's the death threats I object to.'

Former Millwall chairman Reg Burr explains his rules about corresponding with fans of the Lions.

— GREAVSIE'S DEBUT GOALS —

Former England striker Jimmy Greaves is rightly regarded by many pundits as the country's greatest ever goalscorer. A player without obvious weakness, Greaves was quick, sharp, two-footed and nerveless in front of goal. The East Londoner scored on all his senior debuts.

Chelsea v Tottenham Hotspur (White Hart Lane), August 1957
England U23s v Bulgaria (Stamford Bridge), September 1957
England v Peru (Lima), May 1959
AC Milan v Botafogo (San Siro), June 1961
Tottenham Hotspur v Blackpool (White Hart Lane), December 1961
West Ham United v Manchester City (Maine Road), March 1970

— SHIN GUARDS —

The first recorded use of shin guards in English football came in 1874 when players adapted cricket pads to give some rudimentary protection from the heavy boots of their opponents. These early shin guards were strapped on top of the socks but their value was somewhat undermined by the fact that they severely restricted mobility.

— REFS BLOW WHISTLE ON HANKY DAYS —

In football's early days referees had to signal their decisions by waving a handkerchief rather than blowing a whistle. This obviously flawed practice, of course, relied on the players looking in the ref's direction in order to appreciate their sporting semaphore. Salvation thankfully arrived from the unlikely source of Birmingham-based toolmaker Joseph Hudson, who invented the pea whistle in 1860. The new invention was quickly taken up by the police to replace their cumbersome hand rattles. Football soon followed suit, and in 1878 Hudson and Co unveiled the 'Acme Thunderer', a whistle specifically designed for sporting occasions. Hudsons have now manufactured more than 160 million Thunderers.

— WORLD CUP GOLDEN BOOT WINNERS —

1930	Guillermo Stabile (Argentina) **8 goals**
1934	Oldrich Nejedly (Czechoslovakia) **5 goals**
1938	Leonidas (Brazil) **8 goals**
1950	Ademir Marques De Menezes (Brazil) **7 goals**
1954	Sandor Kocsis (Hungary) **11 goals**
1958	Just Fontaine (France) **13 goals**
1962	Drazan Jerkovic (Yugoslavia), Florian Albert (Hungary), Garrincha (Brazil), Leonel Sanchez (Chile), Valentin Ivanov (Soviet Union), Vavá (Brazil) **4 goals**
1966	Eusebio (Portugal) **9 goals**
1970	Gerd Muller (West Germany) **10 goals**
1974	Grzegorz Lato (Poland) **7 goals**
1978	Mario Kempes (Argentina) **6 goals**
1982	Paolo Rossi (Italy) **6 goals**
1986	Gary Lineker (England) **6 goals**
1990	Toto Schillaci (Italy) **6 goals**
1994	Hristo Stoichkov (Bulgaria), Oleg Salenko (Russia) **6 goals**
1998	Davor Suker (Croatia) **6 goals**
2002	Ronaldo (Brazil) **8 goals**

— NICHOLSON'S £1 DISCOUNT —

When Tottenham manager Bill Nicholson signed England striker Jimmy Greaves from AC Milan in December 1961 he successfully and very deliberately negotiated a £1 discount on the fee. The Spurs boss did not want Greaves to be saddled with the burden of becoming English football's first £100,000 player and so paid the Italians £99,999. Greaves had joined Milan from Chelsea six months earlier for a fee of £80,000 and had settled well on the pitch, scoring nine times in 15 games during his Italian sojourn.

— EUROPEAN DERBY —

Prior to the 2003 European Cup final between AC Milan and Juventus, the closest thing to a local derby in a major European final occurred in 1972 when Tottenham Hotspur took on Wolves in the UEFA Cup. The two teams, who are separated by less than 150 miles, met in a two-legged final which Spurs won 3–2 on aggregate. For the record, Milan and Turin are just 90 miles apart.

— THE SAFEST JOB IN FOOTBALL —

The job of football manager is not generally regarded as a secure position offering long-term prospects. There are, of course, exceptions to this rule, and clubs such as Liverpool, Arsenal and Ipswich rarely change their managers. However, the slogan 'safest job in football' would be most appropriately hung over the door of Alan Pardew's office at West Ham United's Chadwell Heath training ground. The Hammers have had just ten permanent managers since their formation in 1895, fewer than any other senior club with the exceptions of Boston United and Rushden And Diamonds, both of whom have far shorter histories. For the record, the list is as follows:

Syd King – Took charge in 1902 when his playing career was cut short by injury. He led the Hammers to the first Wembley Cup final in 1923, and was secretary-manager for 30 years. King's tenure ended tragically when he committed suicide shortly after being suspended by the club for an alcohol-fuelled outburst at a board meeting.

Charlie Paynter – West Ham's long-serving trainer assumed control at Upton Park following King's demise in 1932. He rebuilt the team which had been relegated in 1932, but his progress was hindered by the outbreak of war. Paynter continued in the job until his eventual retirement in 1950.

Ted Fenton – Former player who served his apprenticeship first at Colchester United and then as Paynter's assistant before taking over the reins in 1950. He led the Hammers to promotion in 1958 and earned a reputation for his progressive methods which spawned the famous West Ham academy. Fenton tried to model his team on the great Hungary team of the late 1950s and also gave Bobby Moore his debut. He left the club in the 1960s amid whispers of controversy that have never been elucidated.

Ron Greenwood – The former Arsenal defender became the first 'outsider' to take charge at West Ham and led the club to FA Cup and European Cup Winners' Cup success in the 1960s. Feted for developing the careers of England's World Cup-winning trio of Bobby Moore, Geoff Hurst and Martin Peters, Greenwood moved upstairs to become general manager in 1974.

John Lyall – Greenwood's prodigy took charge in 1974 and led the club to FA Cup success within a year. His eventful tenure also took in two relegations, one promotion, a second FA Cup success and final appearances in both the League Cup and Cup Winners' Cup. His tenure came to an end when his contract was not renewed after relegation in 1989.

Lou Macari – The former Manchester United midfielder became the second outsider to take charge at Upton Park. His reign came to an abrupt end after just seven months amid allegations concerning a betting scandal at former club Swindon Town.

Billy Bonds – The Hammers returned to the tried and trusted after Macari and appointed the club's record-appearance holder Billy Bonds as manager in 1990. Bonds led the club to promotion in his first season in charge. Relegation and a second promotion followed, but Bonds left the club in 1994, insulted by the board's invitation to relinquish his position as manager and become director of football instead.

Harry Redknapp – Assumed control having worked as Bonds' assistant. His charismatic reign saw the club stabilise in the Premiership and even qualify for the UEFA Cup in 1999. Redknapp left the club after a falling out with chairman Terrence Brown in 2001.

Glenn Roeder – Former coach who stepped up to take charge ahead of the 2001–02 season. Guided the Hammers to seventh in his first season, but a year later the club was relegated and Roeder developed a brain tumour that sidelined him for several months. He was sacked after defeat to Rotherham in August 2003.

Alan Pardew – Took charge in November 2003 after a spell as manager at Reading.

— ENGLAND'S GAY NEW FANS —

England's Euro 2004 challenge was given a welcome boost in the run-up to the tournament with the news that the country's ranks of supporters would be temporarily boosted from an unexpected quarter. The homosexual population of Croatia, it seems, have pledged their support to Sven-Goran Eriksson's men in preference to their own national team after comments attributed to manager Otto Baric were interpreted as homophobic. Baric is reported to have said, 'There is no place for homosexuals in my team. Homosexuality is not good.' Gay rights activists reacted angrily to the 71-year-old's comments, with Anto Tomcic explaining, 'We want Croatian football chiefs to do something.' In the meantime, Croatia's lesbians and gays will be backing Becks and the Brits for glory in Portugal.

— TOP BRITS —

At the end of the last millennium the IFFHS (International Federation of Football History and Statistics) carried out a global survey to find the world's best players of the 20th century. Predictably, Pele came first, with Johan Cruyff, Franz Beckenbauer, Alfredo Di Stefano and Diego Maradona, respectively, making up the top five. Bobby Charlton was the top-ranked Briton in the list, and was named tenth. The five other players from the home nations who made it into the top 50 were:

Stanley Matthews (11)
George Best (16)
Bobby Moore (24)
Kevin Keegan (38)
Denis Law (50)

A separate listing for goalkeepers included four Britons, with Gordon Banks finishing the highest, in second place behind Lev Yashin of the Soviet Union. The other Brits honoured were:

Pat Jennings (13)
Frank Swift (26)
Neville Southall (42)

— BEASANT'S BIG DAY —

The FA Cup final of 1988 was a day of firsts. It was Wimbledon's first appearance in the final, and against all odds they beat runaway League Champions Liverpool 1–0 with a goal from midfielder Lawrie Sanchez. It was also the first time a winning team had been captained by a goalkeeper, with the Dons' Dave Beasant lifting the Cup with one glove on and one glove off. (He'd removed his right glove to shake hands with the various dignitaries assembled on the Wembley balcony by the FA.) Beasant had also made history by becoming the first goalkeeper to save a penalty in an FA Cup final when he repelled John Aldridge's goalbound second-half effort. It was the first penalty Aldridge had missed all season, having successfully converted his previous 11.

— 007 ELUDES CAPTURE —

Edinburgh-born Sean Connery was such a proficient footballer in his youth that in 1953 Manchester United manager Matt Busby attempted to sign the future film star, then 23, and make him a Busby Babe. Connery was visiting Manchester as part of the chorus line of the touring *South Pacific* musical when he received the call from Busby after turning out for the *South Pacific* cast against a junior United side. 'It was a great temptation,' said Connery later, after he had decided to focus on acting. It was not the first offer Connery had received to turn professional. A couple of years earlier he had been playing for semi-professional club Bonnyrigg Rose when East Fife offered him a £25 signing-on fee to join them. He turned them down.

Connery, in his days as James Bond, was a frequent visitor to Celtic Park to watch Jock Stein's Lisbon Lions, but by the 1990s he was more often to be seen at Ibrox as a guest of chairman David Murray, who spearheaded Rangers' dominance of Scottish football during that decade.

— QUIRKY KITS —

Football kit is pretty standard fare but, nevertheless, there have been several famous players who have managed to adapt their apparel to bring a little individuality to the field of play:

Jimmy Rimmer (Aston Villa) – rollneck jumper underneath his goalkeeping jersey.

Steve Foster (Brighton, Oxford) – combination of 'big hair' and headband.

Alan Ball (Arsenal) – white boots (in the days before manufacturers made such footwear widely available).

Robbie Fowler (Liverpool) – nasal strips (apparently they make it easier to breathe).

John Barnes (Liverpool) – tights (beneath his shorts).

Dmitri Kharine (Chelsea) – tracksuit bottoms (always).

Thierry Henry (Arsenal) – socks pulled over knees (and not turned over) and gloves.

Paolo Di Canio (Sheffield Wednesday, West Ham and Charlton) – smaller, tighter-fitting shorts than any of his team-mates.

David Beckham/Patrik Berger (Manchester United/Liverpool) – girly headband.

Freddie Ljungberg (Arsenal) – innovative use of hair dye.

— CLOUGHIE'S MIDLAND MIRACLE —

Brian Clough is inarguably among the greatest club managers in English football history. The irascible northeasterner brought unrivalled success to two modest Midlands clubs in the 1970s, taking first Derby County and then Nottingham Forest to League Championships despite limited finances and relatively small squads of players.

Derby had won just one trophy in their 83-year history when Clough arrived in 1967, and memories of that 1946 success in the FA Cup were fading fast. With the help of his able assistant Peter Taylor, he rapidly rebuilt Derby's line-up and in 1972 led them to the Championship. However, Clough was always as controversial as he was inspirational, and he left the Rams in 1973, turning up at near-rivals Nottingham Forest two years later.

Clough led Forest to promotion in 1977 and then to the Championship a year later. A hat-trick of successes was completed in 1979 when Forest beat Malmo in the European Cup final, and, as if to prove that it was no fluke, the Midlanders successfully defended their title the following year. Clough would bring eight major trophies to Forest's City Ground during his 18 years in charge; an impressive record when you consider that they have won no major trophies since and had won only two FA Cups prior to his arrival.

— SOCCER'S HARD MEN —

In 1992 notorious football hardman and soon-to-be Hollywood actor Vinnie Jones provided the voice-over for a controversial video entitled *Soccer's Hard Men*. Unfortunately for Jones, the FA objected to the video's content, which it considered glorified violence in football. Jones, for example, announced to the tape's viewers: 'If you are going to go over the top on me you have got to put me out of the game because I'll be coming back for you; whether it's in the next five minutes or next season.'

Jones was fined a record £20,000 and given a six-month ban which was suspended for three years.

— OFFSIDE CHANGE —

In 1925 the FA attempted to avert a rise in what it considered defensive tactics by changing the offside law to favour the attacking side. The change meant that two rather than three defenders now needed to be ahead of the most advanced attacker for a player to be onside. The FA's efforts proved an instant success, with 1,600 more League goals scored in the first season after the change.

— THE DECLINE OF THE GREAT BRITISH GOALKEEPER —

For most of the 20th century, British goalkeepers were indisputably the best in the world. In the 1960s and 1970s England, in particular, had an embarrassment of luxuries when it came to custodians, with Gordon Banks, Peter Shilton, Ray Clemence, Joe Corrigan and Phil Parkes all vying for the No 1 jersey. The situation began to change in the early 1990s, however, and by the turn of the millennium the status of British goalkeepers had fallen to an alarming low.

The IFFHS compiles annual international rankings of goalkeepers each season, and in the last few years British-born representatives have been few and far between. The most recent available rankings, for 2003, include no Brits at all, with David Seaman the last to make it into a top-ten listing back in 1999. No Briton has topped the list since it began in 1987.

Foreign-born Premiership players, by contrast, have fared rather better. Peter Schmeichel (twice) and Fabien Barthez both topped the list in their respective spells at Manchester United, with the likes of Jerzy Dudek, Brad Friedel and Tim Howard also featuring prominently.

— FOOTBALL LEAGUE RESIGNATION —

According to the Football League's regulations, a club can resign from membership of the League at the end of a season, but must give notice of its intention to do so by 1 January of the year in question. Clubs must then confirm their resignation by 1 April. The exception to this rule is, of course, the promotion of clubs to the Premiership or relegation to the Conference from the League.

— HAIRCUTS FROM HELL —

The Mohican: Otherwise known as a Freddie Ljungberg. Spiky cut for spiky players.

The Skinhead: Becks tried it but never quite managed the 'well 'ard' look. Hammers favourite Julian Dicks was much scarier.

The Mullet or **Bog Brush:** Chris Waddle was among its greatest exponents. Now only seen at dismal '80s theme parties.

The '70s Perm: Step forward Kevin Keegan.

The Hoxton Fin: Another Beckham quiff; another horror show.

The Seaman Pony: Good for flouncing. Won't stop you being lobbed.

The Comb-over: Sad but true. Apparently, Bobby Charlton really did believe it made him look less bald.

THE MOHICAN

THE SKINHEAD

THE MULLET

THE '70s PERM

THE HOXTON FIN

THE SEAMAN PONY

THE COMB-OVER

— TAYLOR MADE —

Sixteen English clubs who have built new stadiums in new locations since 1989*:

Bolton Wanderers – The Reebok Stadium – opened in 1997
Derby County – Pride Park – opened in 1997
Huddersfield Town – The Alfred McAlpine Stadium – opened in 1994
Leicester City – The Walkers Stadium – opened in 2003
Manchester City – The City Of Manchester Stadium – opened in 2003**
Middlesbrough – The Cellnet Riverside Stadium – opened in 1995
Millwall – The New Den – opened in 1993
Northampton Town – Sixfields Stadium – opened in 1994
Oxford United – The Kassam Stadium – opened in 2001
Reading – The Madejski Stadium – opened in 1998
Southampton – St Mary's Stadium – opened in 2001
Stoke City – The Britannia Stadium – opened in 1997
Sunderland – The Stadium Of Light – opened in 1997
Walsall – The Bescot Stadium – opened in 1990
Wigan Athletic – The JJB Stadium – opened in 1999
Wycombe Wanderers – Adams Park – opened in 1990

* Scunthorpe United's Glanford Park opened its doors in August 1988.
** Built for the 2002 Commonwealth Games. Man City moved in the following year.

— THE DUSTBIN FINAL —

The 1960 FA Cup final was dubbed the Dustbin Final by the English sporting press, who roundly condemned the standard of football and refereeing on show at Wembley when Wolverhampton Wanderers and Blackburn Rovers clashed in the season's showpiece. Wolves won the game 3–0 but their cause had been greatly aided by an injury to Rovers' David Whelan, who had broken his leg in a tackle with winger Norman Deeley, who was in the act of scoring the first goal. The Lancastrians were forced to play out the remaining hour with ten men, while their fans spent much of the game howling at the rough tackling of the Wolves and the lenient refereeing of Kevin Howley. The game was also marred by an outbreak of missile throwing from the Rovers fans, who pelted the Wolves players with litter, fruit peel and apple cores on their lap of honour.

— TOP NICKNAMES —

Only the most memorable groups of players are given nicknames but when they are, these tend to resonate down the decades:

The Famous Five was the name applied to Hibernian's exciting forward line of the early 1950s that featured Gordon Smith, Bobby Johnstone, Lawrie Reilly, Eddie Turnbull and Willie Ormond. Their name was lifted from a series of books by author Enid Blyton that featured a group of five friends (*The Famous Five*) and their various adventures. Hibs' Famous Five's escapades included winning the Scottish League title in 1948, 1951 and 1952. Lawrie Reilly was regarded by many observers in the 1950s as the finest centre-forward in Britain, while Ormond became Scotland manager in 1973, leading his country to the 1974 World Cup finals. Turnbull later became Hibernian manager and created another hugely exciting Hibernian team, in the early 1970s, who were themselves nicknamed **Turnbull's Tornadoes**.

Heart Of Midlothian, Hibs' great rivals in Edinburgh, had their own set of favourites in the 1950s: **The Terrible Trio**, which featured Alfie Conn, Willie Bauld and Jimmy Wardhaugh, who spearheaded the Hearts attack as they took the 1956 Scottish Cup, the 1958 League title and the League Cup in 1954 and 1958. Conn's son, also Alfie, would, in the 1970s, win a League title and Scottish Cup medal with Celtic and a Scottish Cup medal with Rangers.

The Wembley Wizards was the nickname applied to the Scottish national team that went to Wembley on 31 March 1928 to face England and, after a magnificent display of the type of instinctive, intricate skills that were intrinsic to the Scottish game at the time, defeated the 'Auld Enemy' by 5–1. The forward line had its own nickname within the nickname of the team, being called **The Wee Blue Devils** on account of their combination of height and trickery. The tallest of them was outside-right Alex Jackson, who stood at 5'10" (1.78m). James 'Ginger' Dunn was 5'6" (1.68m), as was Hughie Gallacher, the centre-forward. Alex James was only half an inch taller than those two, while outside-left Alan Morton was the smallest forward on the field at 5'5" (1.65m) in height. That match at Wembley proved to be the only time that team would play together.

The Lisbon Lions were the eleven players whose inspirational football made Celtic the first British club to lift the European Cup when, on 25 May 1967, they defeated Internazionale of Milan 2–1 in the final of that year's tournament at the National Stadium in Lisbon. The trophy had never previously been won by a club from northern Europe and the odds seemed stacked against Celtic winning on a swelteringly hot afternoon in Portugal, especially when Sandro Mazzola put Inter 1–0 ahead after seven minutes through a penalty. Celtic fought back to overwhelm the Italian side and two exceptional second-half goals, from Tommy Gemmell and Stevie Chalmers, won the match for the Scots, whose progress through the tournament and victory in the final had been masterminded by Jock Stein.

The Lisbon Lions were:

- Ronnie Simpson, the goalkeeper, who, at 36, was the oldest member of The Lisbon Lions. He had begun his career 22 years previously, playing for Queen's Park, and had won FA Cup winner's medals in 1952 and 1955, playing alongside Jackie Milburn for Newcastle United. Jock Stein had, while manager of Hibernian, actually transferred Simpson to Celtic but second time around with Stein, Simpson proved himself an exceptional goalkeeper.

- Jim Craig, the right-back, was 24 at the time of the final. He had been a dental student when he joined Celtic in 1963 and had qualified in 1966. Stein could never understand why Craig could not give up dentistry to focus on football. By the early 2000s he had almost done so, having devoted himself almost entirely to his work with Celtic's in-house media team.

- Tommy Gemmell, the left-back, and 23 in Lisbon, scored an exceptional long-range goal in the final, one of 64 in his career at Celtic, many of which were equally spectacular. His shot was once measured at more than 70 miles per hour (113kph). He later managed Dundee and Albion Rovers and currently works in the financial services industry.

- Bobby Murdoch, the right-sided midfielder, was 22 and the man who made the team tick with his exceptional passing skills and vision. His pass set up Chalmers' winning goal in Lisbon. He managed Middlesbrough in the 1970s but tragically became the first Lisbon Lion to pass away, in 2001.

— TOP NICKNAMES (CONT'D) —

- Billy McNeill, the centre-back and captain, 27 in Lisbon, was an inspirational leader and a dominant figure in the air. He lifted the European Cup on his own in Lisbon after a pitch invasion made it impossible for any other players to accompany him to its presentation. He later became manager of Aberdeen, Manchester City, Aston Villa and of Celtic, twice. He currently undertakes media work.

- John Clark, the sweeper, 26 at the time of the final, was a steadying influence in the team. He later became assistant manager to Billy McNeill at Aberdeen and Celtic, and managed Cowdenbeath, Clyde and Stranraer. He returned to Celtic as kit man in 1997, a position he continues to hold.

- Jimmy Johnstone, the outside-right, was the fans' favourite. A small, red-haired, exceptionally skilful and tricky winger, he was 22 in Lisbon and, as a hugely entertaining figure, would soon be renowned worldwide for his skills. He made a total of 67 appearances for Celtic in European competition, a figure bettered only by Billy McNeill with 72. Sadly, Johnstone was diagnosed with motor neurone disease in the early 2000s, a condition against which he battles bravely.

- Willie Wallace, the inside-right, was 26 at the time of the final and the only member of the team to have been signed during that 1966–67 season, arriving from Heart Of Midlothian for £28,000 in December 1966, with Celtic narrowly beating Rangers in the race to sign him. Following his football career, he emigrated to Australia in the 1980s to run sports shops.

- Stevie Chalmers, the centre-forward, was 30 at the time of the 1967 European Cup final. His place in the team had been under threat when Willie Wallace was purchased by Jock Stein, but an injury to top scorer Joe McBride in December 1966 offered Chalmers a reprieve that culminated in him scoring the winner in Lisbon five minutes from time. He now works as a corporate hospitality host for Celtic.

- Bertie Auld, 29 in Lisbon, stunned the Italians by leading his team-mates in renditions of Celtic songs in the players' tunnel prior to the final. He and Murdoch went on to push and pull the game in Celtic's direction. Auld spent a lengthy career in football management, most prominently at Partick Thistle and Hibernian, and is now a corporate hospitality host for Celtic.

- Bobby Lennox, 23 at the time of the European Cup final, was a pacy forward whose 273 goals for Celtic make him the club's highest goalscorer since World War II and second only to the great Jimmy McGrory, who scored 472 goals for the club in the 1920s and 1930s. Lennox currently helps organise player representation for corporate hospitality at Celtic.

— PARKING SPACE —

Football League clubs must provide at least four parking spaces for directors of the visiting club at all matches.

— FOOTBALL LEAGUE CAPACITY —

The criteria for Football League membership includes stipulations about the minimum ground capacities for competing clubs. A newly qualified member (ie clubs promoted from the Conference) must have a stadium that holds at least 4,000 seated supporters, of whom 500 must be under cover. Clubs must also show they have the ability to increase their capacity to 5,000 (with 1,000 under cover) and must do so by 31 May of their first season in the League. After three seasons in the League all member clubs must have a minimum overall capacity of 5,000 (2,000 under cover).

— BUTCHER ON SOUNESS —

'The gaffer [Graeme Souness] makes everyone sit down and then goes through his comments on the first half. "Right, you bastards," he says, or sometimes stronger if we're not playing well.'

Terry Butcher recalls Souness's inspiring half-time pep talks in his book Both Sides Of The Border.

— VILLA WIN NEW CUP —

The League Cup was born in 1961 and was the brainchild of the Football League's secretary, Alan Hardaker. The first competition began during the 1960–61 season but because of fixture commitments the final was not contested until the start of the following campaign, with Aston Villa beating Rotherham 4–3 on aggregate over two legs.

The first League Cup final to be contested in a one-off match at Wembley came in 1967 when Queens Park Rangers defeated West Bromwich Albion 3–2. The Londoners were a Third Division side at the time and caused a famous upset by coming from 2–0 down against their First Division rivals to clinch a late but deserved victory.

The 1967 final had been made even more interesting because, for the first time, a European place was at stake. The League had negotiated automatic Fairs Cup qualification for the winners, providing they were a First Division team. QPR were, of course, not a top-flight side, so missed out on this additional prize.

A SELECTION OF FOOTBALLERS WHO HAVE EACH WON THE EUROPEAN CUP/CHAMPIONS LEAGUE — WITH TWO DIFFERENT CLUBS —

Miodrag Belodedici.....Steaua Bucharest (1986); Red Star Belgrade (1991)
Marcel Desailly ....Marseille (1993); AC Milan (1994)
Didier Deschamps..................................Marseille (1993); Juventus (1996)
Vladimir Jugovic ....Red Star Belgrade (1991); Juventus (1996)
Ronald Koeman ....PSV Eindhoven (1988); Barcelona (1992)
Saul Malatrasi..................................Inter Milan (1965); AC Milan (1969)
Christian Panucci ....AC Milan (1994); Real Madrid (1998)
Frank Rijkaard ....AC Milan (1989); Ajax (1995)
Dejan Savicevic ....Red Star Belgrade (1991); AC Milan (1994)
Clarence Seedorf ....Ajax (1995); Real Madrid (1998)
Paolo Sousa...........................Juventus (1996); Borussia Dortmund (1997)

— MOORE THE CENTURION —

England's World Cup-winning skipper Bobby Moore made his 100th senior international appearance in the 5–0 win over Scotland at Hampden Park on Valentine's Day 1973.

— HILL TAKES THE FLAG —

On 16 September 1972 Jimmy Hill stepped down from his position in the commentary box at Highbury to take over the duties of an injured linesman during a League match between Arsenal and Liverpool. Hill, a qualified referee, volunteered to run the line after Dennis Drewitt was unable to continue. The match ended in a goalless draw, but without Hill's intervention it would have been abandoned.

— FOOTBALL LEAGUE TIMELINE —

1885	Professionalism legalised
1888	Football League founded
1898	Promotion and relegation introduced
1939	Player numbers introduced on shirts
1951	White ball makes its debut
1956	First floodlit game (Portsmouth v Newcastle United)
1960	League Cup launched
1961	Maximum wage removed
1965	Substitution allowed for the first time (but only for injured players); tactical substitutions allowed a year later
1981	Three points for a win introduced
1982	League Cup sponsored; name changed to Milk Cup
1983	League Championship sponsored by Canon
1987	Play-offs introduced (for promotion and relegation)
1992	First Division breaks away to form the Premier League

— TWO CLOSE FOR COMFORT —

The Scottish national team's worst two successive defeats in peacetime internationals came in the 2003–04 season, with Berti Vogts, a World Cup winner with West Germany in 1974, as manager: a 6–0 loss in Amsterdam to Holland in the second leg of a European Championship play-off and a 4–0 defeat from Wales in a friendly in Cardiff. There was a Scottish connection among the scorers in both matches. Frank De Boer, who scored the fifth goal in Holland's win, would join Rangers from Galatasaray two months later, in January 2004. Robbie Earnshaw, who notched a hat-trick for Wales in Cardiff in February 2004, had played for Morton in the 1999–2000 season, when he had lived above a pub in Greenock.

— JOE FAGAN —

Former Manchester City centre-half Joe Fagan was a true footballing all rounder, enjoying success as a player, a trainer and as a manager. The Liverpool-born defender was among a generation of players whose careers were affected by the outbreak of war in 1939, but Joe did not let such global-political problems scupper his rise to the very pinnacle of the game. He was 18 when war was declared against Germany and as a result of the suspension of League football in 1939, he did not make his senior debut until he was 25.

With the exception of three appearances for Bradford Park Avenue, Joe played out his professional career with City before returning to Merseyside to become a key member of Liverpool's famous Boot Room. He remained somewhat in the background at Anfield during the reigns of Bill Shankly and Bob Paisley, but his low media profile belied his value to the club, where his skills not only as a coach but also as a 'trainer' were highly valued. In the 1960s and 1970s clubs did not always have a medically trained physio, but instead employed a trainer (usually a former player) with practical qualifications and expertise in football injuries and their treatment.

Bob Paisley had fulfilled a similar role at Anfield prior to his elevation to the post of manager in 1974, and so when Paisley retired, with a record that was then arguably the most successful in English football history, the Liverpool board opted to employ a like-for-like replacement. Fagan was the man to fill the breach, though at 62 he was the oldest managerial debutant in League history. He was also a reluctant hero and needed to be encouraged to take the position. Despite his reservations and a certain amount of media reticence, Joe proved an instant success, leading Liverpool to the League title, the League Cup and the European Cup in his first season in charge. The next season proved rather less glorious, but Joe had already decided to retire prior to the end of a trophyless campaign that will forever be remembered for the Heysel stadium disaster in which 39 people died.

— BIG JACK HONOURED —

In 1994 the former England defender and World Cup winner Jack Charlton was made a Freeman of the City of Dublin in honour of his achievements as manager of the Republic Of Ireland. In nine years in charge, Big Jack guided the Boys in Green to the 1988 European Championships finals and two World Cup tournaments (1990 and 1994).

— ENGLAND'S MANAGERS —

For its first 67 years, England's international team was selected by the FA and coached by a variety of guest trainers. However, in 1946, following a disappointing 1–0 defeat against Switzerland in Zurich, the FA's secretary, Stanley Rous, decided the time was right for change. Rous promoted England's chief coach Walter Winterbottom to become the country's first full-time manager.

Walter Winterbottom...1946–63
Alf Ramsey 1963–74
Joe Mercer...1974
Don Revie...1974–77
Ron Greenwood 1977–82
Bobby Robson...1982–90
Graham Taylor 1990–93
Terry Venables 1994–96
Glenn Hoddle...1996–99
Howard Wilkinson 1999, 2000
Kevin Keegan 1999–2000
Peter Taylor...2000–01
Sven-Goran Eriksson 2001–

— ITALIA '90 TRIGGERS FOOTBALL RENAISSANCE —

Following the successes of both England and the Republic Of Ireland at the 1990 World Cup finals, the domestic game in Britain embarked on something of a renaissance in popularity in the early 1990s. A decline in hooliganism at grounds, which was widely credited to improved policing and a shift in trends in popular culture, also contributed to football's rising stock. Football was suddenly fashionable again and the opening day of the 1990–91 season attracted the highest total attendance for eight seasons.

— ALF GARNETT ON THE HAMMERS —

'We're friendly down at West Ham. We like to go out into other divisions, an' meet other teams, an' brighten their lives a little, an' entertain 'em to what is the quality of attractive football.'

Alf Garnett explains West Ham United's unique place in the pantheon of English football, Daily Mirror, *1980.*

— CANTILEVER PIONEERS —

The first cantilever stand (you know the ones, the angled stands that don't have annoying pillars holding them up) was erected at Scunthorpe's Old Show Ground stadium in 1958. Sheffield Wednesday soon followed suit with a similar structure replacing the club's East Stand in 1962.

— POLL-WINNING REF —

Graham Poll is England's top referee according to the annual referees' poll conducted by the IFFHS in 2004. The Hertfordshire official came tenth in the international rankings, which were topped by Italy's Pierluigi Collina for the sixth year running.

WORLD'S BIGGEST CLUB, AVERAGE CONDITION, — GOOD PROSPECTS – £10M ONO —

In 1989 Manchester United's majority shareholder, Martin Edwards, agreed to sell his controlling interest in the club to Michael Knighton for just £10 million (plus guarantees that a further £10 million would be spent developing the club's stadium). The deal later fell through; something for which Edwards would be eternally grateful. When he finally sold the bulk of his shares in the early years of the new century, their value had reportedly risen to more than £75 million.

— NAMES FOR THE GAME —

- Rangers were named after an English rugby union club.
- Irish-Catholic priests founded Hibernian and adapted the Latin name for Ireland, *Hibernia*, when naming the Edinburgh club.
- Celtic's founders, in contrast to those who founded Hibernian, were keen not to identify the club entirely with Ireland even though its followers were mainly Irish. They named the club Celtic so that Scots could also identify with it as a club for all Celts.
- Queen Of The South is the only football club whose name can be located in the Bible; at Luke 11:31 in the New Testament: 'The Queen of the South shall rise up in the judgement with the men of this generation and condemn them.'

— KICKING AREAS OF THE BOOT —

It might seem obvious but you'd be surprised how many regular players don't work at *how* they kick the ball. This diagram shows the four basic striking points – the instep (for short, straight side passes), the inside (for imparting right-to-left spin and swerve on a shot or floated pass), the laces (for a driving shot or fast pass) and the outside (for left-to-right swerve). Dead easy...which is why you'll *never* see a pro kicking a direct free-kick ten yards wide!

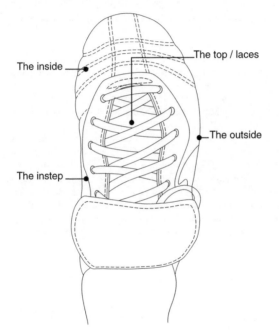

The inside

The top / laces

The outside

The instep

TOFFEEMEN BEST-SUPPORTED CLUB
— IN NEW LEAGUE —

During the first season of League football in England, Everton were the best-supported team in the competition, drawing average crowds of around 7,000 to their home games during that 1888–89 season. Today, more than a century later, the Toffeemen are the seventh best-supported team in the Premiership, with average gates of around 38,500. Manchester United, with around 67,500, top the list.

— MEAGAN BLAZES A TRAIL —

The Republic Of Ireland's first permanent manager was former Everton defender Mick Meagan, who took charge of the Boys in Green for 12 games between 1969 and 1971. Meagan's appointment had been backed by the players, who championed the claims of the veteran defender while calling for an end to the outmoded and ineffective process by which the team was chosen by an FAI (Football Association of Ireland) selection committee.

Unfortunately, Meagan's reign could not bring an end to the chaos that had long dogged the Irish national team. Internationals were invariably scheduled for Sundays which meant English-based players had to turn out for their club sides on a Saturday and then get themselves to Dublin the same evening. Travel problems, injuries and late withdrawals were frequent, and Meagan recalls that headcounts were usually needed to see which of the selected players had made it in time. Indeed, on one occasion the manager himself had to make a quick trip home to get his boots in order to make up the numbers.

The net result was that Meagan's teams were frequently filled with inexperienced players from League Of Ireland clubs. Unsurprisingly, the Republic's form during his tenure was, to put it mildly, unimpressive, and when his 12th game in charge ended in a 4–1 defeat against Austria at Dalymount Park the FAI dismissed him. With disarming honesty, Mick recalls: 'It was a great opportunity to stay involved with the lads on a more or less full-time basis. But in two years we didn't win a game and, while we had faced tough opponents in every match, they [the FAI] were right to bring in somebody new.'

— KILLER UPDATE —

'God knows what was wrong with him. When we get him home, we'll put some scaffolding round him and have a look.'

Oldham boss Joe Royle gives the media an update on the fitness of giant defender Brian 'Killer' Kilcline.

— MEXICO 1970 —

The 1970 World Cup finals in Mexico were the first to be broadcast live and in colour in Britain.

— BORO BREAK BRITISH BOSS HOODOO —

Steve McClaren became the first English manager to win a major trophy in eight years when he led Middlesbrough to League Cup success over Bolton Wanderers at Cardiff's Millennium Stadium in February 2004. The last success by an English boss had come when Brian Little led Aston Villa to the same trophy (see page 118). Boro's 2004 success was also the first time the Teesside club had won any major silverware in their 128-year history.

— WORLD CHAMPIONS XI (PLUS 2 SUBSTITUTES) —

A team of non-English World Cup winners who have played in Britain:

Fabien Barthez (Manchester United)
Marcel Desailly (Chelsea)
Emmanuel Petit (Arsenal, Chelsea)
Frank Leboeuf (Chelsea)
Patrick Vieira (Arsenal)
Didier Deschamps (Chelsea)
Osvaldo Ardiles (Tottenham Hotspur, Blackburn Rovers, Queens Park Rangers, Swindon Town)
Jose Kleberson (Manchester United)
Christophe Dugarry (Birmingham City)
Youri Djorkaeff (Bolton Wanderers)
Gilberto Silva (Arsenal)

Subs: **Juninho** (Middlesbrough)
Jurgen Klinsmann (Tottenham Hotspur)

— A SAD DEMISE —

Third Lanark are the only Scottish League title winners to be no longer in business. They won the Scottish title in the 1903–04 season but went bust in 1967. The club's full name was the Third Lanarkshire Volunteer Reserves – they had originally been the sporting section of a military regiment. Their stadium at Cathkin, Glasgow, remains intact if in a state of some disrepair.

— THE ACADEMY OF FOOTBALL —

Highbury may be known by some as the 'Home of Football' and Manchester United's Old Trafford ground may be the 'Theatre of Dreams', but the title of the 'Academy of Football' belongs to one of English football's most enigmatic clubs. West Ham United earned the moniker in the 1960s but, contrary to popular belief, the tag has nothing to do with the club's reputation for developing local talent. In fact, the 'Academy' was a nickname given to a group of like-minded senior players who were brought together during Ted Fenton's time as manager at Upton Park and who all went on to enjoy high-profile managerial careers themselves.

The Academy's unofficial but undoubted leader was the charismatic football modernist Malcolm Allison, a man with a voracious appetite for learning about the tactics, professionalism and style of continental European teams. Allison would meet with team-mates who included Ken Brown, John Bond, Noel Cantwell, Dave Sexton and Frank O'Farrell in a café yards from Upton Park and would spend hours discussing tactics, formations and practice drills after training.

Fenton accepted (or at least tolerated) the ideas of the Academy members, and Allison's influence, in particular, became increasingly apparent in training sessions. The club's youngsters also benefited from the progressive ideas of Allison and co, who helped coach schoolboy players including Bobby Moore, Geoff Hurst and Martin Peters in the evenings.

When their own playing days were at an end, the Academy graduates wasted little time embarking on managerial careers at the top level of the game. Neither before nor since have so many future coaches played in the same team.

ACADEMY GRADUATES
Malcolm Allison – Plymouth Argyle (1964–65 and 1978–79); Manchester City (1972–73 and 1979–80); Crystal Palace (1973–76 and 1980–81); Middlesbrough (1982–84); Bristol Rovers (1992–93)

John Bond – AFC Bournemouth (1970–73); Norwich City (1973–80); Manchester City (1980–83); Burnley (1983–84); Birmingham City (1986–87); Shrewsbury Town (1991–93)

Ken Brown – Norwich City (1980–87); Plymouth Argyle (1988–90)

Noel Cantwell – Coventry City (1967–72); Peterborough United (1972–77 and 1986–88)

Frank O'Farrell – Torquay United (1965–68 and 1981–82); Leicester City (1968–71); Manchester United (1971–72); Cardiff City (1973–74)

Dave Sexton – Leyton Orient (1965); Chelsea (1967–74); Queens Park Rangers (1974–77); Manchester United (1977–81); Coventry City (1981–83)

— KAMARA STRIKES HISTORIC BLOW —

In January 1988 Swindon midfielder Chris Kamara became the first professional footballer to be fined in a criminal court for an assault on an opponent in a game. Kamara was fined £1,200 for grievous bodily harm after he broke the jaw of Shrewsbury Town's Jim Melrose.

— FROM DOLPHINS TO SEAGULLS —

Brighton & Hove Albion are widely known as the Seagulls but the nickname is a relatively new one, and its adoption came about in somewhat bizarre circumstances. According to footballing folklore, a group of Brighton fans began chanting the name in reaction to Crystal Palace fans who had been howling their own 'Eagles' chant at them across a crowded pub prior to a Brighton v Palace 'derby' game at the Goldstone Ground in the mid-1970s. The club duly took note and the official badge, which had only been redesigned to incorporate a dolphin three years earlier, was appropriately reworked.

— STADIUM SAFETY —

The Taylor report of 1989 was the ninth official inquiry into ground safety and crowd control at football matches in Britain. Among the previous reports were the findings of commissions that had followed the Ibrox Stadium disaster of 1972, in which 66 supporters died in a crush on an exit stairway, and the Valley Parade fire of 1985, in which 56 fans died. The Taylor report was, of course, commissioned in response to British football's worst stadium disaster at Hillsborough on 15 April 1989 when 96 fans died and hundreds were injured by crushing at the FA Cup semi-final between Nottingham Forest and Liverpool. The report would find that the disaster had been caused by poor crowd management by the police and inadequate facilities.

— LEAGUE OF IRELAND CAPS —

A team of Republic Of Ireland internationals who have won caps while playing their club football for League Of Ireland sides:

Paddy Roche (Shelbourne)
Shay Brennan (Waterford)
Paddy Mulligan (Shamrock Rovers)
Tommy McConville (Dundalk, Waterford)
John Giles (Shamrock Rovers)
Mick Martin (Bohemians)
Joe Haverty (Shelbourne)
Liam O'Brien (Shamrock Rovers)
Ray Treacy (Shamrock Rovers)
Mick Leech (Shamrock Rovers)
Mick Lawlor (Shamrock Rovers)

— 'THE FA' NOT 'THE ENGLISH FA' —

The Football Association is known as the FA and not the English FA, a move which indicates the organisation's status as the original association and a driving force in the development of the modern game.

— LAWTON MAKES SHOCK MOVE —

In 1947 Third Division Notts County pulled off one of the most surprising transfers in British football history by signing the England centre-forward Tommy Lawton for a record fee of £20,000 from Chelsea. Lawton duly became the first player from outside the top two divisions to play for England.

— TEA-TIME TURN OFF —

When ITV outbid the BBC for the FA Premiership highlights rights in 2000, they took the bold decision to bring the programme forward in the schedules from its usual 10:30pm slot (as established by BBC's *Match Of The Day*) to 7pm and the weekend's prime position. The BBC's late-evening programme had enjoyed an average of 4 million patrons each week, but at 7pm ITV's *The Premiership* would need to see that audience grow to around 7 million to justify the move. Unfortunately for ITV the switch had a detrimental rather than a positive effect on viewing figures. When the audience fell to a low of just 3.2 million the programme was, with a certain inevitability, returned to its familiar position in the listings and, with no less predictability, the missing viewers returned (presumably from the pub with a take-away) to their sofas and TV sets.

— BECOMING A REFEREE —

According to footballreferee.org (the official website of the Referees' Association), there are 20,000 active referees in England at present. To become a referee, you must be over 14 years of age, be reasonably fit and have good eyesight (with or without glasses or contact lenses). Anybody who fulfils these criteria can go on one of the free referee training courses which are run locally by training officers at branches of the Referees' Association. Courses last for nine weeks and are classroom based. Trainees must pass two assessments before they are eligible to take charge of their first local match. Referees under the age of 16 are only permitted to officiate at youth-level matches.

— THAT LEFT-SIDED PROBLEM —

Since the early 1990s England have had a well-documented problem finding a left-sided midfielder to take charge of the shirt formerly worn by the likes of Chris Waddle, John Barnes and Peter Barnes. A succession of England managers have wrestled with the problem but none have found a convincing solution. Among those to have 'had a go' on the left wing for England in the last 12 years are:

Eleven No 11s

Tony Dorigo

Steve McManaman

Paul Scholes

Nicky Barmby

Joe Cole

Frank Lampard

Trevor Sinclair

David Dunn

Kieron Dyer

Emile Heskey

Owen Hargreaves

— GIRLS RECOGNISED BY ESFA —

It took until 1990 for the ESFA (English Schools Football Association) to formally recognise that girls play football. The ESFA duly rewrote its constitution to reflect this fact.

— THREE DAYS OF NON-STOP ACTION —

On the weekend of 18/19 August 2001 the *Guardian* kept a record of all televised football available to British audiences with access to both terrestrial and satellite reception. Including the 165 minutes of Sky Sports pay-per-view games screened, footie fans were free to gorge themselves on 4,275 minutes (or three solid days) of action.

so they must have nicked it from its original setting – namely the 1945 Broadway musical *Carousel*. How many working-class Rodgers and Hammerstein fans were there in Glasgow in the 1940s?

Celtic
For one thing, Celtic arguably pioneered the idea of mass singing on the terraces – and we're not just talking about nasty jibes at the British monarchy. A 1926 edition of *The Glasgow Observer* mentions the 'thunderous chorus' of Irish favourites such as 'Hail Glorious St Patrick', 'God Save Ireland' and 'Sleivenamon'. It's surely not beyond the bounds that they'd know the hits from *Carousel*. Look, Sunderland has a proud working-class fan base but The Stadium Of Light can still hum along to *Ride Of The Valkyries*.

Perhaps both sets of fans should just get over it and start practising 'Walk On By'.

— POSH GETS THUMBS UP FROM BECKS —

'It's a nice thumb to be under... it could be a horrible, nasty thumb.'

David Beckham quips back as reporters suggest he is under his wife's thumb.

— OLD HANDS —

The oldest professional player to make his English League debut is believed to be centre-half David Donaldson, who was aged 35 years and 8 months when he turned out for Wimbledon on 22 August 1977 – also the Dons' League debut in what was the old Fourth Division.

Manchester City favourite Tony Book was also something of a codger – 28 is virtually pensionable these days – when he made his first League appearance for old Second Division side Plymouth Argyle back in 1964.

However, records like these are made to be broken. Put your money on any handy-looking Conference side with a 36-year-old goalie!

— ITALIAN JOB —

The first English professional to play in Italy was Herbert Kilpin, considered one of the fathers of Italian soccer. Born in Nottingham in 1870, he was a regular for FC Torinese by his 21st birthday and later played for Mediolanum Milano (1898–1900) and Milan (1900–07).

Kilpin's finest hour came on 16 December 1899 when he and some fellow expats persuaded businessman Alfred Edwards to help finance a team to be known as the Milan Cricket And Football Club. The idea was to play as much cricket as possible while promoting the game of football at every opportunity. Nowadays the club is better known as AC Milan.

According to the AC Milan online website, the idea came while Kilpin and his pals were 'at a pint'. The *Guardian* has it that they were in a Tuscan wine shop. This tells you all you need to know about European stereotyping.

Anyway, Edwards went on to become the first president, and Kilpin was in the side that beat his old team Mediolanum 3–0 in an inaugural fixture. The MCFC teamsheet that day contained a handful of Brits, with names such as Lees, Neville and Allison all featuring.

— MUST-KNOW FACT —

West Brom goalkeeper John Osborne – a Baggies hero in the '60s – had a plastic knuckle. It never affected his performance, and until 2002 he jointly held the club record for most clean sheets in a season – 22.

— SO IT WAS ALWAYS LIKE THIS THEN? —

'Any team moving from the Second Division to the First needs half a million pounds spare to buy players. The club must also have an average home gate of at least 30,000, because the First Division is in effect two divisions in one: the elite, and the rest who make up the numbers.'

Dave Bowen, Northampton Town manager, 1966

— GOAL DROUGHTS —

The former Liverpool full-back Rob Jones is often cited as a player who couldn't score. While it's certainly true that the England international never once found the back of the net in 243 appearances for Liverpool, it's fair to say that he was particularly unlucky, hitting the woodwork with agonising regularity and often coming a cropper during attacking runs into his opponents' penalty box.

Goal-shyness is by no means uncommon in professional football and the name of one other – now retired – player comes to mind as a long-term sufferer. Respect, please, though to Steve Whitworth, the stalwart defender who played 399 times for Leicester City between 1969 and 1979. In all those matches Steve scored just the once, although it was a good 'un. So good, in fact, that it won the 1971 Charity Shield – securing a 1–0 win over Liverpool and giving City's backroom staff a rare opportunity to break out the Brasso. Still, Whitworth didn't have to wait as long as Francis Benali, who scored his one and only goal for Southampton in his 11th season with the club (1997–98). Still, better late than never!

— JUST CHAMPION —

Only one team has ever won the European Cup (as it was then called) more times than its own domestic League competition. The feat was accomplished by little old Nottingham Forest who, in the late 1970s, marshalled by the brilliant Brian Clough, outplayed the continent's biggest names with some fearless attacking football. For the record, Forest won the old First Division in 1977–78, lifted the European Cup in 1979 and then retained that trophy the following year.

— GLASS ACT —

These days it's not unusual to see a goalkeeper turn makeshift striker for a last-minute jolly into the opposing penalty area. But few goalies have transformed themselves quite so effectively and dramatically as Carlisle's Jimmy Glass. His role in the events of Saturday, 8 May 1999 was the stuff of *Boys' Own* fiction. Except you couldn't have made this up.

Only a Carlisle fan could properly explain the depth of frustration – almost malevolence – hanging over Brunton Park that afternoon. The previous season the club had been relegated from Division Two. Now it was about to drop out of the Nationwide League altogether. Nothing less than a home win against Plymouth would do – and yet the team had played abysmally all season.

The thought of Cumbria losing a third League side (Workington and Barrow had both succumbed during the 1970s) was haunting United fans' every waking moment. Many blamed chairman Michael Knighton for the club's woes, accusing him of being tight-fisted. Earlier that week Knighton had announced a £1.4 million operating profit, proof in his eyes that Carlisle enjoyed sound stewardship. Predictably, the fans would rather have blown the lot on new players.

In fact, Carlisle had a good first half against Plymouth. Only when the visitors' 18-year-old starlet Lee Phillips scored a fine individual goal did the black mood descend with a vengeance – first through dead silence; then via a stream of invective aimed at Knighton. This febrile atmosphere was relieved briefly when Stuart Whitehead hit a 25-yard equaliser, but with every passing minute United edged closer to the abyss. As the clock ticked into injury time, 7,500 fans steeled themselves for the drop and the heartache of non-league obscurity. Then Carlisle won a corner.

Both sides packed the Argyle penalty box as the lone figure of Jimmy Glass raced up from the far goal mouth, moving faster – though only just – than home fans heading for the exits. The corner swung in; Scott Dobie headed on, the 'keeper's punch was poor and suddenly, gloriously, Glass found the ball at his feet. He buried it. Carlisle had been saved with the final kick of the final second of the final game…by their 'keeper's first ever League goal.

The ensuing pitch invasion by 3,000 delirious fans took several minutes to clear. Briefly, there was the horrific thought that the match might have to be abandoned and replayed. Fortunately for United the ref blew for kick-off and then almost immediately for full time.

It was a good party in Carlisle that night. However, sadly, the club's fortunes have shown little sign of an upturn. As the 2003–04 season drew to a close they faced yet another torrid relegation battle.

LAMBERT GIVES A HELPING HAND — TO THE GERMANS —

Paul Lambert became the first British footballer to win the European Cup with a continental club when he helped Borussia Dortmund lift the trophy in 1997.

— BALL PLAY —

Ever wondered how the FA allocates numbers to clubs for its Cup draw? Here's what happens:

In the first round, all the Division Two and Three teams are numbered in alphabetical order from 1–48, with the likes of Bristol Rovers getting a single figure and Yeovil Town up there in the 40s. Numbers 49 and above are then allocated to non-league sides in the order they come through the fourth qualifying round. All clear so far?

When Premiership and First Division sides enter the fray in the third round they are allocated available numbers alphabetically, together with all victors from second-round matches. Any clubs forced into a replay are given a number based on the order in which they eventually make it through.

However, from the fourth round onwards, teams are numbered according to when they were drawn out of the hat – or glass bowl – in the previous round. So, to sum up, if your club is Middlesbrough and you're the first name out in the fourth-round draw, and you win your tie, then you will be Number 1 for the fifth-round draw. Got it? No? Let's move on.

— WINNING PERCENTAGES —

This is a statto's heaven. The chart shows the percentage of wins in a team's entire history, covering every League game, up until the start of the 2003–04 season. If you hadn't done the research you'd probably guess at roughly half and half for the oldest clubs. And you'd be right. Still, bragging rights go to Liverpool.

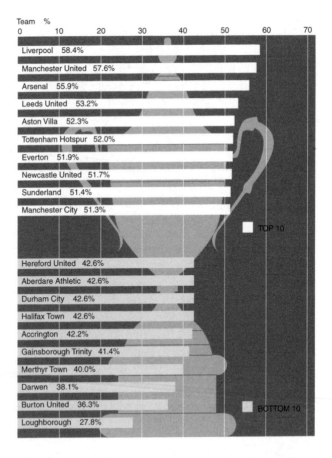

Team %

Team	%
Liverpool	58.4%
Manchester United	57.6%
Arsenal	55.9%
Leeds United	53.2%
Aston Villa	52.3%
Tottenham Hotspur	52.0%
Everton	51.9%
Newcastle United	51.7%
Sunderland	51.4%
Manchester City	51.3%

☐ TOP 10

Team	%
Hereford United	42.6%
Aberdare Athletic	42.6%
Durham City	42.6%
Halifax Town	42.6%
Accrington	42.2%
Gainsborough Trinity	41.4%
Merthyr Town	40.0%
Darwen	38.1%
Burton United	36.3%
Loughborough	27.8%

☐ BOTTOM 10

— NEIGHBOURS FROM HELL —

In 1909 the Division One title went to Newcastle United, but not before the Magpies endured one of the lowest points in their illustrious history. When Newcastle hosted neighbours Sunderland at home in the League that season, there was nothing to suggest the home side's high standards would be compromised. Newcastle were gunning for the League title, which they held in 1907 but had let slip through their fingers in the subsequent year. At half time the scoreboard showed the teams drawing 1–1.

But in the second half, all hell broke loose in the Newcastle half. Sunderland put away eight goals within 28 minutes, the last five scored in just eight minutes. Two Sunderland players, Billy Hogg and George Holley, notched up hat-tricks. After the 9–1 drubbing Newcastle players withdrew to lick their wounds.

Showing remarkable powers of recovery, however, Newcastle came out to win ten out of their next 11 matches to secure the Division One top spot. In the Cup that year they beat Sunderland 3–0 at Roker Park, following a 2–2 draw at St James' Park. (The FA Cup was eventually won by Manchester United that year, after beating Bristol City 1–0 in the final.)

— SPORT OF KINGS —

The first reigning monarch to watch an FA Cup final was King George V (reigned 1910–1936) in 1914, a few short months before the outbreak of World War I. The venue was the Crystal Palace, London's premier sporting arena at the time. Burnley were playing Liverpool, with both sides struggling to find form in the League. Ultimately Burnley came away victorious following a 58th minute goal, and captain Tommy Boyle received the Cup from the king, who was among 72,000 spectators.

— LIKE FATHER LIKE SON —

A team (plus one sub) of sons with accomplished footballing fathers.

Father	Son
Johan Cruyff	Jordi
Ian Wright	Shaun Wright-Phillips
Brian Clough	Nigel
Kenny Dalglish	Paul
Phil Mellor	Neil
Alex Ferguson	Darren
Frank Lampard	Frank Jnr
Finn Laudrup	Brian
Terry Owen	Michael
Harry Redknapp	Jamie
Alec Herd	David
Arnor Gudjohnsen	Eidur

— LIKE FATHER AND GRANDFATHER, LIKE SON —

Only one entry among the pro ranks (er, we think). Raise a glass to the Summerbee family, which can boast three generations of Manchester City players: grandfather George, father Mike and son Nicky.

— MATCH-FIXING SCANDAL —

The year 1915 is best remembered for trench torment, failed offensives and thousands of army casualties. News of the war kept the scandal of match fixing in football that erupted that year very much on the inside pages. Yet it was a shocking story of collusion designed to fleece the bookies of hundreds of pounds. News of it first broke when accusations were printed on handbills and distributed by a firm of bookmakers. In response to calls for an inquiry, the Football League established a committee of investigation, which reported back some nine months later.

The match in question was between Manchester United and Liverpool. Bookmakers had been alerted when an unusual number of wagers were placed on United winning 2–0. The FA found that four players on each side were guilty of conspiring to fix the match and all were given a life ban from playing football. The Liverpool four were Tom Fairfoul, Tommy Miller, Bob Purcell and Jackie Sheldon. Those in the United ranks were Laurence Cook, Sandy Turnbull, Arthur Whalley and Enoch 'Knocker' West. Curiously, Cook, Turnbull and Whalley did not play in the match at all. Sheldon, a former United player, was said to have been the go-between for the scam. West was the only player who did not have the life ban lifted after the war. By some quirk, the result was permitted to stand.

But they were not the only English football players to make wrong choices during the era. Before the war, Steve Bloomer was England's most prolific goal scorer. He retired in 1914 and decided on a coaching career in Germany. Before he carried out so much as a warm-up he was interned by the Germans and remained so for the remainder of hostilities.

— DOOLEY'S DISASTER —

As the football season came to a close in 1952, Sheffield Wednesday were relishing the prospect of clashing with England's soccer giants after becoming Division Two Champions. Hero of the hour was Wednesday centre-forward Derek Dooley, who scored 46 goals in 30 League matches.

Imagine, then, the horror when first Dooley broke his leg in a match against Preston on Valentine's Day 1953 trying to put a ball past the 'keeper and then had to have the damaged limb amputated after gangrene set in. Dooley, aged just 23, was a sure-fire bet for an England shirt before the tragedy.

— SCOTLAND IN THE WORLD CUP —

Qualification for the finals of the World Cup is today seen as of vital importance, but it was not always so. In 1950, FIFA had stated that they would allow the countries that finished first and second in the British Home International Championship to contest the World Cup in Brazil that summer. Scotland finished second after losing their final match 1–0 at home to England, but because they had failed to win the Home International Championship, the Scottish Football Association refused to allow the players to participate in the finals. After the match at Hampden, England captain Billy Wright had pleaded with George Young, his counterpart in the Scottish team, to ask the SFA to reconsider their decision. Young did so but the SFA refused to budge.

Scotland would go on to qualify for the first time in 1954 and between then and the eighth time they qualified, in 1998, they had one of the best World Cup-qualifying records in the world. Their record of qualifying for the finals from the group stages was bettered only by Italy and equalled only by Brazil and Germany. Unfortunately, on arrival at the finals, things have often come undone for the Scots:

— SCOTLAND IN THE WORLD CUP TIMELINE —

1954

In 1954, for their first World Cup finals, in Switzerland, the SFA decided that Scotland would take just 13 players to the finals even though tournament regulations allowed squads of 22. It meant that the Scots only had one goalkeeper: Fred Martin of Aberdeen. After their opening match, a 1–0 defeat by Austria, manager Andy Beattie resigned, disillusioned by interference from SFA officials in his work. Scotland subsequently suffered their record defeat in their second match, when they were beaten 7–0 by Uruguay.

1958

Matt Busby of Manchester United agreed to manage the Scots in their second tournament in Sweden in 1958, but as a result of injuries he sustained in the Munich disaster in February of that year he was unable to go to Sweden with the squad. The SFA decided not to appoint a replacement for Busby and, amid suggestions of indiscipline among the players in Sweden, Scotland tumbled out of the tournament with just one point from their three group games.

1974

At the 1974 tournament, Scotland were, for the first time, the only representatives from the British Isles and were desperately unlucky to become the first country ever to be unbeaten but still find themselves eliminated from the finals. Goal difference was the Scots' downfall. After beating Zaire 2–0 and drawing with group rivals Brazil and Yugoslavia, Scotland went home because they had scored one goal fewer than Brazil, after the Brazilians, in their final match, got a lucky late goal to defeat Zaire 3–0.

1978

Scotland travelled to Argentina for the 1978 finals with the most talented squad in the country's history. It featured, among its many illustrious names, 1978 European Cup winners Kenny Dalglish and Graeme Souness of Liverpool and 1978 Football League winners Archie Gemmill, Kenny Burns and John Robertson of Nottingham Forest. Burns was England's Player Of The Year and Gordon McQueen, one of four Manchester United players in the squad, was Britain's most expensive player. Ladbrokes had Scotland at 8–1 to lift the trophy before the tournament began, but a 3–1 defeat to Peru in the opening match was exacerbated by winger Willie Johnston's sample proving positive at the post-match doping test.

FIFA stated that Fencamfamin, a psycho-motor stimulant, and a drug banned by FIFA, had been found in Johnston's sample. Johnston was only the second player in World Cup history, after Ernst Jean-Joseph of Haiti in 1974, to be found guilty of taking a banned substance. FIFA had the power consequentially to eject Scotland from the World Cup, so the Scottish Football Association had to be seen to take strong action and Johnston was sent home.

Scotland was stunned and morale reached rock bottom after a 1–1 draw with Iran that saw Scottish supporters in Argentina turn viciously on ebullient manager Ally MacLeod. The Scots rallied and finally found their form with a fine 3–2 victory over Holland in their final group match, but yet again they were eliminated from the finals on goal difference.

— SCOTLAND IN THE WORLD CUP TIMELINE (CONT'D) —

1982

A 20,000-strong Scottish support followed the team to the south of Spain for their group matches in the 1982 World Cup. After being 3–0 up against New Zealand in their opening match, Scotland allowed the Kiwis to get two goals back before winning 5–2. Scotland, now managed by Jock Stein, also opened the scoring in their next match, against Brazil, when David Narey sent a wonderful 20-yard shot high into the Brazilian net, but Scotland went on to lose 4–1, then drew 2–2 with the Soviet Union in their final match. For the third successive tournament, the Scots found themselves eliminated on goal difference, with the loss of those goals against New Zealand making the difference between elimination and qualification for the next round.

1986

A pall of gloom was cast over the qualifying stages for the 1986 World Cup finals in Mexico when Jock Stein, the Scotland manager, collapsed and died after suffering a heart attack in the final minutes of the 1–1 draw with Wales in Cardiff on 10 September 1985. Alex Ferguson took over from Stein for the finals and although Scotland lost to Denmark and Germany in their opening matches, they entered their third group match, with Uruguay, with the chance of progressing, if they were to win. French referee Joel Quiniou took the dramatic step of dismissing Uruguay's José Batista after a foul on Gordon Strachan in the opening minute, but subsequently allowed himself to be intimidated by the South Americans, their violent approach going unchecked thereafter. It ended 0–0 and Scotland left for home with the normally sedate SFA secretary Ernie Walker calling the Uruguayans 'the scum of world football'.

1990

Scotland began their fixtures in the 1990 finals with one of the most embarrassing defeats in their history, going down 1–0 to Costa Rica, who were playing their first-ever match in the World Cup finals. Boos from 10,000 Scottish supporters hounded Scottish manager Andy Roxburgh to the dressing room but he revived the team to defeat Sweden, one of the tournament favourites, in classic Scottish battling style, only to be eliminated by a late goal in a 1–0 defeat by Brazil.

1998

The 1998 World Cup in France found Scotland participating in the opening match of the tournament for the first time, when they faced holders Brazil in front of 80,000 at the Stade de France. The ceremonials were spectacular and Scotland were holding the Brazilians to a 1–1 draw when Tom Boyd put through his own goal to gift Brazil the winner. It was, overall, a generally encouraging start but the Scots, managed by Craig Brown, then drew 1–1 with Norway and collapsed against Morocco, losing 3–0 and tumbling out of the tournament at the group stage for the eighth consecutive time.

— NO JOB IS SAFE —

There's an old joke that says that football managers should get themselves to the Job Centre sharpish if they hear their club chairman pledging personal support. But let's hear it for the club chairmen who are inadvertently caught short with management changes. Ossie Ardiles may or may not have been heartened by the words of Newcastle chairman Sir John Hall when he stuck up for the diminutive Argentinian, under pressure after only 11 months in the post, as Newcastle wobbled at the wrong end of Division Two in 1992.

'Let's kill off once and for all the rumours that Ossie's job is on the line. If he leaves the club, it will be of his own volition.' (2 February 1992)

Imagine his surprise when Ardiles was unceremoniously sacked within days and Kevin Keegan, English football's first millionaire, was installed in his place.

'I feel absolutely dreadful about what has happened… when I said those words, I meant each and every one of them.' (5 February 1992)

Hall failed to explain why he didn't know about the monumental changes that were afoot in his beloved club. But hey, this is football. Anything can happen.

— GREATEST SOCCER CITY —

Given that London has historically had the most Premiership or First Division clubs you'd think it would be a shoo-in for the title UK Soccer Cup Capital. Indeed, London is top of the tree but the race is surprisingly close.

For this battle to be fair there ought to be some kind of weighting – a Tottenham League Cup, for instance, really shouldn't count the same as a European Champions League trophy. Still, we haven't got time for all that, so here's the crude, hard cup count. Charity Shield wins are excluded because these would skew everything still further.

LONDON

Arsenal	25
Tottenham	16
Chelsea	8
West Ham	4
Wimbledon	1
Charlton	1
QPR	1
Total	**56**

LIVERPOOL

Liverpool	38
Everton	15
Total	**53**

MANCHESTER

United	29
City	9
Total	**38**

— HOME GROWN —

Given that overseas players now rule the Premiership it's heartening to recall that the Celtic European Cup-winning team of 1967 was composed entirely of Glaswegians (see pages 49–50).

— LOVE THY NEIGHBOUR —

Three sets of local derby grounds which lie uncomfortably close to each other:

1. Anfield and Goodison Park, separated by Stanley Park.

2. City Ground, Nottingham (home of Forest) and Meadow Lane (home of County), separated by the River Trent.

3. Dens Park (Dundee) and Tannadice Park (Dundee United) located on either side of Tannadice Street.

— WORLD CUP HICCOUGHS —

Everyone remembers England's victory in the 1966 World Cup competition. But how many can recall what happened four years before and after the triumph. In 1962 the contest was played out in Chile and the Cup was retained by Brazil after the South American supremos defeated Czechoslovakia 3–1. (The scorers were Amarildo, Zito and Vava, Pele being out with an injury.) England were beaten by Brazil in the quarter-finals, in a match that ended with the same scoreline. In 1970, in Mexico, England were again defeated in the quarter-finals, this time by West Germany, who scored three goals to England's two. Brazil were victorious in a five-goal thriller against Italy. Pele, Gerson, Jairzinho and Carlos Alberto scored for Brazil, while Boninsegna tucked one away for beaten finalists Italy.

— BORN STARTER —

Having provided the first goal in the reigns of Glenn Hoddle (against Moldova) and Sven-Goran Eriksson (against Spain) for England, Nick Barmby was the first scorer of the ill-fated Terry Venables era at Leeds United (against Manchester City).

TOTAL NUMBER OF GOALS CONCEDED BY 'KEEPERS (ACTIVE AND RETIRED) IN THE HISTORY OF THE — PREMIERSHIP TO THE END OF JANUARY 2004 —

Ian Walker 422

David James......................................384

Neil Sullivan 362

Tim Flowers......................................354

Nigel Martyn 340

Kevin Pressman..................................311

David Seaman 295

Peter Schmeichel 289

Paul Jones 288

Neville Southall..................................281

In fairness to those at the top of the net-bulging league, you have to ask how old Safe Hands would have managed behind the Leicester City defence or whether Schmeichel would have been quite so good playing for Wimbledon. And surely goals conceded per game would be a better guide. Still, things aren't fair in football. Which duly makes poor old Ian Walker the worst goalie ever to pull on a Premiership shirt.

— THREE OF A KIND —

Only three teams have won the Premiership trophy since it replaced the old First Division title in 1992–93. None have been managed by an Englishman.

1. Manchester United (Alex Ferguson): 1993, 1994, 1996, 1997, 1999, 2000, 2001, 2003

2. Arsenal (Arsène Wenger): 1998, 2002

3. Blackburn Rovers (Kenny Dalglish): 1995

— EVER PRESENTS —

Of the original 22 clubs that comprised the first-ever Premiership, nine have contested every season to date. They are: Manchester United, Arsenal, Liverpool, Chelsea, Leeds United, Aston Villa, Tottenham Hotspur, Everton and Southampton.

Oldham Athletic have fared the worst of the original line-up, dropping to the Second Division and almost going out of existence in 2003.

— SUBBUTEO FACTFILE —

- **Subbuteo** is apparently the Latin name for a bird of prey called the Hobby.

- After the success of the football game, **Peter A Adolph** made companion games for various sports, including rugby, cricket, speedway, fishing and even five-a-side football.

- Subbuteo figures were painted by hand (for the most part in **Tunbridge Wells**) until 1977.

- There are several references to Subbuteo in pop music, with the most notable coming from Northern Ireland punk band **The Undertones** in their 1980 single 'My Perfect Cousin', which featured the immortal line: 'He always beat me at Subbuteo, cos he flicked the kick and I didn't know...'

— EUROPEAN CUP PIONEERS —

Hibernian were Britain's first representatives in European football when they contested the inaugural 1955–56 European Cup tournament. They reached the semi-finals before going down to Stade de Reims of France. The two legs of their tie with Djurgardens of Sweden were played in Scotland because of weather conditions in Sweden, with the 'away' leg being played at Firhill Stadium, Glasgow, the home of Partick Thistle. Hibs won 1–0 at home and 3–1 'away'. The European Cup at that time was supposed to be reserved strictly for League Champions but Hibernian had actually finished the previous season in fifth position in the Scottish League.

— OFFICIAL HAND SIGNALS —

Goal

Red (sending off) or yellow (booking) cards

Play on. The ref is indicating no offence or allowing advantage (ie there's been a foul but the wronged team has already moved into a better position)

Indirect free-kick

Goal kick

Corner kick

Penalty kick

Team wins throw-in (flag points to the goal they're attacking)

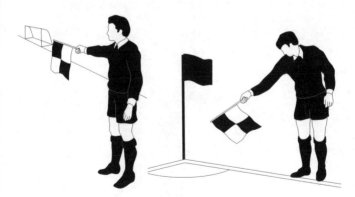

Goal kick

Corner kick

Offside

Foul spotted

Substitute waiting

— KEEP RIGHT ON —

Birmingham City's fan base enjoyed something of a resurgence in the 16 years the club spent outside the top flight from the mid 1980s. Successive matches staged at St Andrews at this level drew 6,234 (against Arsenal in May 1986) and 28,563 (against Blackburn Rovers in August 2002).

— GETTING DOWN —

Two League clubs have suffered the ignominy of relegation in three successive seasons, both spiralling downwards in the days before the Premiership was born:

Bristol City (1980–82), Wolves (1984–86)

In the 1977–78 season, West Ham United had Trevor Brooking on the pitch and won six of their last nine games but were relegated from the old First Division. In 2002–03, with Brooking as the caretaker manager for the final couple of weeks, they won six of their last 11 matches and still went down.

— COME OFF IT —

Most supporters believe they make better offside calls than the assistant referee. According to *Nature*, the scientific journal, they may well be right. While preparing a paper for publication, Dr Raoul Oudejans gave officials 200 offside situations to assess, using youth teams playing games to a script. Forty of them were misjudged because of an optical illusion that gave the impression of the player farthest away from the official being closer to goal. Testing their theory by watching video footage of European Championship and World Cup matches, Oudejans and his colleagues discovered that strikers on the far side of the pitch were nearly nine times more likely to be wrongly judged offside than if they ran past the defender on the side nearer the assistant referee. So it's not a myth – you really can see the whole thing better while sitting in the stands.

— ENGLAND'S IRE —

When Brian Little led Aston Villa to the Coca-Cola Cup in 1996, he became the last English manager to lift a domestic trophy for eight years. Scotland and France dominated the spoils until Steve McClaren broke his duck and won the Carling Cup with Middlesbrough in 2004.

1996

FA Carling Premiership, FA Cup ....Alex Ferguson
(Manchester United, Scotland)
Coca-Cola Cup ....Brian Little (Aston Villa, England)

1997

FA Carling Premiership...Alex Ferguson
(Manchester United, Scotland)
FA Cup...Ruud Gullit (Chelsea, Holland)
Coca-Cola Cup...Martin O'Neill
(Leicester City, Northern Ireland)

1998

FA Carling Premiership, FA Cup ....Arsène Wenger
(Arsenal, France)
Coca-Cola Cup.............................Ruud Gullit (Chelsea, Holland)

1999

FA Carling Premiership, FA Cup ....Alex Ferguson
(Manchester United, Scotland)
Worthington Cup ....George Graham
(Tottenham Hotspur, Scotland)

2000

FA Carling Premiership..Alex Ferguson
(Manchester United, Scotland)
FA Cup ....Gianluca Vialli (Chelsea, Italy)
Worthington Cup...Martin O'Neill
(Leicester City, Northern Ireland)

2001

FA Carling Premiership ....Alex Ferguson
(Manchester United, Scotland)

FA Cup, Worthington Cup ......Gerard Houllier (Liverpool, France)

2002

FA Barclaycard Premiership, FA Cup ....Arsène Wenger
(Arsenal, France)

Worthington Cup ..Graeme Souness (Blackburn Rovers, Scotland)

2003

FA Barclaycard Premiership ....Alex Ferguson
(Manchester United, Scotland)

FA Cup ....Arsène Wenger (Arsenal, France)

Worthington Cup ....Gerard Houllier (Liverpool, France)

2004*

Carling Cup ....Steve McClaren (Middlesbrough, England)

---

* As at March 2004

— IT'S NOT CRICKET —

The highest score recorded in Scottish football, and for a first-class match, was Arbroath's 36–0 defeat of Bon Accord in the Scottish Cup first round on 12 September 1885. There was a good explanation for the result. The team that took the field under the name of Bon Accord was actually Orion Cricket Club, who had been invited to participate in the competition in error: the invitation should have gone to Orion Football Club. The cricketers, despite arriving in Arbroath without any football equipment, gamely took to the pitch for the resultant thumping. It could have been worse for them: Mr David Stormont, the referee, disallowed half a dozen other goals.

— SING WHEN YOU'RE WINNING —

Five half-decent football-related songs of the modern era...

'World In Motion' ....New Order, 1990
'Three Lions' ....Baddiel, Skinner and
The Lightning Seeds, 1996
'England's Irie'......................................Black Grape, 1996
'Touched By The Hand Of Cicciolina'..........Pop Will Eat
Itself, 1990
'Eat My Goal' ....Collapsed Lung, 1996

...and five best left to gather dust.

'Anfield Rap'......................................Liverpool FC, 1988
'Ossie's Dream' ....Tottenham Hotspur FC/
Chas 'n' Dave, 1981
'This Time (We'll Get It Right)' ..England World Cup squad,
1982
'Blue Day' ....Suggs and Co, featuring Chelsea, 1997
'Don't Come Home Too Soon'...............Del Amitri, 1998

— BREAK WITH HISTORY —

The breakaway formation of the Premier League, or Premiership, in 1992, marked the beginning of a new era in football history. Founded by the Football Association after years of heated debate, the new-look top flight owed its establishment largely to pressure from the leading clubs, who saw the opportunity to better their financial footing and, in doing so, improve the state of the game at the top level at least. Key to these plans was the involvement of BSkyB, the multi-national satellite television organisation.

BSkyB's owner, Rupert Murdoch, sanctioned a £304 million payment for a five-year rights deal on the new competition, guaranteeing clubs like Manchester United around £3 million a year – a hundred-fold increase on the previous arrangement with the Football League. Although the fee was regarded as staggering at the time, Murdoch has since referred to the Premiership as the 'battering ram' that got pay TV off the ground in the United Kingdom.

The League was reduced from 22 to 20 teams in 1995, in the hope that the new organisation would offer the chance to relieve overcrowded fixture lists and allow the national team more time for preparation (although this plan failed to foresee a proliferation in international friendlies and European club competition). One of its other main aims, at which it can claim largely to have succeeded, was to keep the best British players at home and attract foreign stars. But for all its perceived benefits, clubs in the lower divisions were particularly opposed to the Premiership, fearing that they would be starved of funds by the elite teams, though it was promised that cash would be directed to less prestigious sides.

Initially it seemed as though the Premiership was really just the old First Division armed with a new television deal, plus the addition of green shirts for referees and linesmen (as they were then known). But the money behind the scenes was making a massive difference, enabling clubs to combine the cost of building merchandising and catering centres with the all-seater safety standards demanded in the wake of the Hillsborough disaster. With England's performance in the 1990 World Cup, when they reached the semi-finals, still fresh in the mind of potential fans, football quickly regained the popularity it had lost in the previous decade. The foundations were in place for what would become the most-watched League in the world.

— YELLOW FEVER —

How can a team that lasted one season in the Premiership top the table more than a decade after they were relegated? Easy – it's a disciplinary table, and Swindon Town lead the field. The Wiltshire club accrued just 44 cards from their 42 matches – but while one booking or sending-off per game might not make the Robins whiter than white, most other clubs average two. Would a more physical approach have served Swindon well? We'll never know...

— CROWD PLEASERS —

Hampden Park boasts having played host to three of Europe's record attendances:

1. On 17 April 1937 it was filled by the largest crowd ever to attend an international game in Europe when 149,547 were drawn to the match between Scotland and England; an estimated 10,000 more gained entry without paying and the vast majority of the crowd were delighted to see the Scots defeat the Auld Enemy 3–1.

2. One week later, on 24 April 1937, the largest attendance for any club match anywhere in Europe filled the ground, when 146,433 saw Celtic defeat Aberdeen 2–1 in the Scottish Cup final. Approximately 20,000 more were unable to gain entry. Willie Buchan scored the winning goal for Celtic 20 minutes from time and, as he left the pitch, he might have expected to receive hearty congratulations. Instead, the first person to greet him was a Celtic director who harangued Buchan for winning the match for Celtic when a draw would have ensured a replay with another mammoth crowd and commensurate gate receipts.

3. Celtic moved their 1970 European Cup semi-final with Leeds United from their own Celtic Park to Hampden Park because demand for tickets was so great. Tickets went on sale to the public three and a half weeks before the match and within two hours they had all been sold. On the night, a crowd of 136,505 packed the terraces with thousands more gate-crashing the affair. Celtic won 2–1 to reach the final.

— LIKE FOR LIKE —

Denis Law, a proud Aberdonian, was the first Manchester United player ever to be substituted, when he left the field of play after sustaining a knee injury at White Hart Lane in a match with Tottenham Hotspur in October 1965. His replacement was John Fitzpatrick, another Aberdonian.

— PREMIER TEAMS —

The Premiership table at the end of the competition's first season, 1992–93, read:

	PLAYED	POINTS
Manchester United	42	84
Aston Villa	42	74
Norwich City	42	72
Blackburn Rovers	42	71
Queens Park Rangers	42	63
Liverpool	42	59
Sheffield Wednesday	42	59
Tottenham Hotspur	42	59
Manchester City	42	57
Arsenal	42	56
Chelsea	42	56
Wimbledon	42	54
Everton	42	53
Sheffield United	42	52
Coventry City	42	52
Ipswich Town	42	52
Leeds United	42	51
Southampton	42	50
Oldham Athletic	42	49
Crystal Palace	42	49
Middlesbrough	42	44
Nottingham Forest	42	40

— TAIT THREE —

The first-ever hat-trick in the English Football League was scored by Walter Tait, who on 15 September 1888 scored three of Burnley's four goals in their 4–3 away win at Bolton – the second weekend of the League's existence. It was a shining moment in an otherwise unremarkable season for his club. Burnley finished ninth out of twelve.

— ANORAK-LOVERS ONLY —

Like over-zealous steam train enthusiasts and stamp collectors, football fans who drone endlessly on about team formations should really be locked away as a public nuisance. If you do get trapped by one, best pretend you're deaf and dumb. Failing that, stick to the absolute basics as follows:

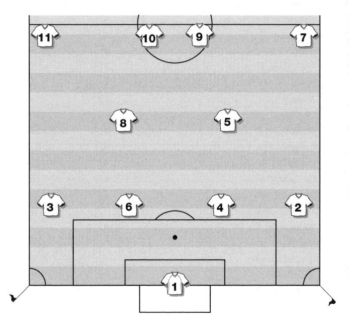

4–2–4: Decidedly untrendy nowadays because few sides can spare the luxury of full-time wingers who won't mix it in midfield. Still, if your team plays this way you should see plenty of goals.

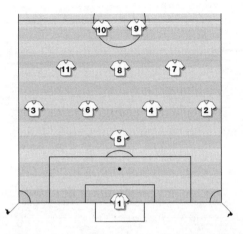

Catenaccio: Those damned cunning Italians came up with this one. Play two up front, rely on fast counter-attacking, score one goal and pack the defence and midfield for football's equivalent of trench warfare. Not pretty, but effective.

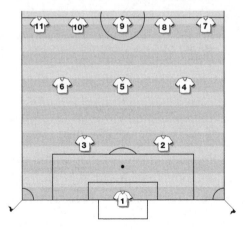

2–3–5: In the good ol' days, this was how you set up your Subbuteo players. No messing about, everyone with a clear job and all positions with a proper name. True bliss. The only problem was that as footballers got better, 2–3–5 didn't.

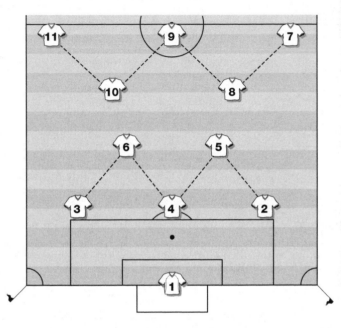

WM: The idea was that your two attacking midfielders linked with your forwards and your two defensive midfielders linked with your defenders and all the midfielders linked with each other and...oh what's the point, we lost 6–3 to Hungary using this one.

— LUCKY SEVEN —

Just a handful of players have managed 350 or more appearances in the Premiership:

PLAYER	CLUBS IN THE PREMIERSHIP
Gary Speed	Leeds United, Everton, Newcastle United
Alan Shearer	Blackburn Rovers, Newcastle United
Teddy Sheringham	Nottingham Forest, Tottenham Hotspur (twice), Manchester United, Portsmouth
Ryan Giggs	Manchester United
Gareth Southgate	Crystal Palace, Aston Villa, Middlesbrough

Nigel Winterburn.................................Arsenal, West Ham United
David James.................Liverpool, Aston Villa, West Ham United,
Manchester City

Of the above, only Gary Speed has played more than 400 Premier League games.

— GROWING OLD DISGRACEFULLY —

The success of other, more prestigious, competitions has without doubt removed some of the shine of the League Cup, despite the fact that it still offers its winner a guaranteed UEFA Cup place for the following season. Yet it should be remembered that the competition, founded in 1960, had to effectively re-invent itself with the advent of football sponsorship in the early 1980s, so, much like one might expect of a dysfunctional child, a period of instability was inevitable. This notion is reflected in the Cup's portfolio of backers: from its suckling years as the Milk Cup (1982–86), through the adolescent times of the Coca-Cola Cup (1993–98), to the hard-drinking, difficult times of the Worthington Cup (1999–2003) and Carling Cup (2004). Between 1987 and 1992 the competition was sponsored first by Littlewoods, then by Rumbelows, which just goes to prove how unpredictable youngsters can be.

— IT'S A GAME OF MIXED METAPHORS —

'I can drink like a chimney.'

– *Duncan Ferguson*

'If you can't stand the heat in the dressing room, get out of the kitchen.'

– *Terry Venables*

'He [the Anderlecht player] hits it into the corner of the net as straight as a nut.'

– *David Pleat*

— IT'S A GAME OF MIXED METAPHORS (CONT'D) —

'[His] white boots were on fire against Arsenal and
he'll be looking for them to reproduce tonight.'
  – Ron Atkinson

'These managers all know their onions and cut their
cloth accordingly.'
  – Mark Lawrenson

'We never took the game by the scruff of the neck.
We didn't take them to the cleaners – that would
have been the icing on the cake.'
  – Glenn Hoddle

'I can see the carrot at the end of the tunnel.'
  – Stuart Pearce

'The tide is very much in our court now.'
  – Kevin Keegan

— OUT OF THEIR LEAGUE —

Since the 1986–87 season, a system of automatic relegation has been in
place for teams finishing bottom of the League (replacing re-election, the
previous lifeline afforded to wooden-spoon winners). During that time, 12
different clubs have endured the drop into non-league football, with the
champions of the Nationwide Conference (previously GM Vauxhall
Conference) taking their place in the League. Lincoln City was the first to
go, but the club regained its berth the following season by winning the
Conference. The bottom clubs in the Fourth Division were not relegated in
1990–91 and 1991–92, because a decision had been taken to restore the
old First Division to 22 teams, and on three occasions in the 1990s, the
Conference winners – Kidderminster Harriers, Macclesfield Town and
Stevenage Borough – missed out on promotion because their grounds were
deemed unfit for League football. A two-up, two-down system was
introduced in 2002–03, raising the stakes even higher for struggling League
clubs and their ambitious stalkers...

SEASON	RELEGATED	REPLACEMENT
1986–87	Lincoln City	Scarborough
1987–88	Newport County	Lincoln City
1988–89	Darlington	Maidstone United
1989–90	Colchester United	Darlington
1990–91		Barnet
1991–92		Colchester United
1992–93	Halifax Town	Wycombe Wanderers
1993–94, 1994–95, 1995–96		
	No promotion or relegation	
1996–97	Hereford United	Macclesfield Town
1997–98	Doncaster Rovers	Halifax Town
1998–99	Scarborough	Cheltenham Town
1999–2000	Chester City	Kidderminster Harriers
2000–01	Barnet	Rushden And Diamonds
2001–02	Halifax Town	Boston United
2002–03	Exeter City	Yeovil Town
	Shrewsbury Town	Doncaster Rovers

— SPOT ON WITH STOREY —

'It was all very well them leaping about and going mad, but I had to stick the ball in the net. And against Gordon Banks...'

Arsenal penalty taker Peter Storey recalls his team-mates' elation at being awarded an injury-time spot-kick against Stoke City in the FA Cup semi-final of 1971.

— HARDEST GAME IN THE WORLD —

The game may be faster, the haircuts sillier, and all manner of silky skills on show for Saturday afternoon punters, but football continues to produce its fair share of hard men. Here are five of the most notorious:

— HARDEST GAME IN THE WORLD (CONT'D) —

JOHN FASHANU

English forward who spearheaded the Wimbledon side that became one of the dominant teams in the First Division in the late 1980s. Began his career with Norwich City and later appeared for Crystal Palace, Lincoln City and Aston Villa, but it was the South London 'Crazy Gang' with which he was most associated. Boasting strength and tenacity, at times he was among the most effective strikers in the League, and he became a hero of Wimbledon's supporters.

ROY KEANE

It is debatable whether Manchester United would have enjoyed anything like their success of the 1990s and early 21st century without Roy Keane, a genuinely world-class player as well as hard man. Finest hour at club level was his performance in the European Cup semi-final of 1999, when he rallied United from two down to beat Juventus 3–2 in Turin, only to miss the final against Bayern Munich because of suspension. Fined £150,000 and banned for five matches in 2002 after admitting to deliberately injuring Alfie Haaland, an opponent in the 2001 Manchester derby.

VINNIE JONES

A former hod-carrier, Jones transferred from Wealdstone to Wimbledon in 1986 and subsequently established himself as one of the most notorious players in the League. Moved to Leeds United in 1989 and also played for Sheffield United and Chelsea before returning to Wimbledon. Sent off six times in six years, Jones received a £20,000 fine and six-month ban from the FA in 1993 after featuring in *Soccer's Hard Men*, a video advising how to commit professional fouls (see page 44). Now a successful Hollywood actor.

MARK DENNIS

Although best remembered in the Southampton colours of the mid '80s, Dennis also played for Birmingham City, Queens Park Rangers and Crystal Palace. Despite an uncompromising style, he was one of the best left-backs in the country at the time and played a major role in Southampton's successful 1983–84 season, when the club finished runners-up in the old First Division and reached the semi-final of the FA Cup. Enjoyed something of a reputation off the pitch too, hence his most memorable moment: 'Getting stabbed by my ex-wife.'

PATRICK VIEIRA

Arsenal's answer to Roy Keane, Vieira marshals the Highbury midfield every bit as well as his Old Trafford rival, but early in his career he threatened to walk out on English football because of 'unfair' treatment at the hands of referees. Vieira, also a member of the most successful France side in history, was once fined £45,000 after being sent off for a foul on Paolo Di Canio and then spitting at Neil 'Razor' Ruddock – both of whom had their own no-nonsense reputations – in a Premiership match against West Ham United in 1999.

None of the above can match Bert Trautmann, Manchester City's legendary goalkeeper. He broke his neck in the 1956 FA Cup final and carried on playing. Now that's hard!

— NAME GAMES —

There are four clubs among the 92 that comprise the Football League starting and ending in the same letter. They are Charlton Athletic, Aston Villa, Liverpool and York City. (Spurs doesn't count because it is a nickname.) On a similar note, Arsenal is alphabetically the first in the Football League while York City is bottom. After Halifax and Exeter endured the drop, only two Nationwide League clubs have the letter x in their names and they are Wrexham and Crewe Alexandra. A quick analysis of the League also reveals that some English counties are under-served by Premier or Nationwide League divisions. Shropshire, Cornwall, Surrey, Huntingdonshire and Hereford were five counties without a team in the top-flight divisions during the 2003–04 season. It is worse in Wales, as just three clubs (Cardiff, Swansea and Wrexham) out of 92 represent the principality.

— FREE AND EASY —

Wanting to leave his club, FC Liège in 1990, Jean-Marc Bosman, the Belgian footballer, was forced to take his employers to the Belgian courts and then to the European Court of Justice. As a result of his case the 'Bosman Ruling' was confirmed in 1995. It barred transfer fees for players out of contract and removed limits on the number of foreign players allowed at individual clubs, the latter ruling because of a contravention of Articles 48 and 85 of the Treaty Of Rome.

The consequences of the Bosman ruling were that professional football could no longer be regarded as extra-territorial or above Community law. So, on 19 February 1996, UEFA, the European football governing body, was forced to abolish all restrictions on the number of players from European Union member states who could play for European clubs and do away with all conditions (especially financial conditions) linked to the transfer of players at the end of their playing contract between clubs in European Union member states.

The end of the 1996 season, following the shop-window for international players provided by the European Championship (Euro '96) in England, saw a large number of top players moving club. Either they were out of contract and were able to offer their services free of transfer – and therefore negotiate far higher wages from a new club – or clubs were more inclined to sell players and claim a transfer fee before the contract ran out. Probably the most notorious 'Bosman' in English football was that of Sol Campbell, who moved from Tottenham Hotspur to Arsenal for free in 2001.

— CELEBRITY CARES —

Lots of football clubs enjoy the support of well-known stars of stage and screen. Here are ten that may surprise you:

STAR	OCCUPATION	CLUB
Tom Hanks	Actor	Aston Villa
Alan White	Drummer with rock band Oasis	Charlton Athletic
Leonard Cohen	Singer–songwriter	Chelsea
Jenny Seagrove	Actress	Everton
Prince William	Second in line to the throne	Aston Villa
Shania Twain	Singer–songwriter	Tottenham Hotspur
David Shayler	Former MI5 spy	Middlesbrough
Jackie Chan	Actor	Arsenal
Robert Plant	Led Zeppelin superstar	Wolverhampton Wanderers
Stefan Edberg	Retired tennis legend	Leeds United

— THERE CAN BE ONLY ONE —

One club has dominated the first 12 years of the Premiership – Manchester United – and although the title has not always been theirs, its fate has been decided by whichever team has best kept up with the men from Old Trafford. Perhaps surprisingly, there have been some exciting title fights.

Blackburn Rovers finished a single point ahead of United to win their sole Premiership title, in 1994–95. Newcastle United, under the management of Kevin Keegan, looked to have the Championship wrapped up the following season: but then came a loss of confidence and some clever psychology from Sir Alex Ferguson, and the Tyneside team ended up four points adrift.

Arsenal have been best at keeping pace with United in recent years. Arsène Wenger led them to their first Premiership trophy in 1997–98, beating their rivals into second place by one point. United gained their revenge the following season, this time triumphing over Arsenal – again, by a single point. The North London club won the title again in 2001–02, but towards the end of the following campaign they suffered a similar fate to that of Newcastle seven years earlier and ended up five points behind United.

— THERE CAN BE ONLY ONE (CONT'D) —

Despite the excitement of the Premiership, the most memorable finish in history actually occurred in 1988–89 – three years before the new competition was formed. United, who were still regrouping in Ferguson's early years, were not even involved.

The battle for the title was between Liverpool and Arsenal and, as luck would have it, these two contested the last match of the season at Anfield. If Arsenal won by two clear goals, the title would go to Highbury by virtue of a superior goal difference. Although they managed to go 1–0 up, George Graham's team looked doomed to finish second as the clock ticked into added time – until the 92nd minute, when Michael Thomas stuck the ball into the back of the net and won the old First Division Championship with the last kick of the season. So ended the most exciting title race of all time, a drama so perfect in its execution that it spawned Nick Hornby's book *Fever Pitch*, and a film of the same name.

— A STREET APART —

Dundee and Dundee United are the two clubs closest to each other geographically in British senior football. Dundee's Dens Park and Dundee United's Tannadice are situated on the same street, Tannadice Street, and are only 100m (110 yards) apart. The two clubs would have become even closer if the joint Scotland/Ireland bid to host Euro 2008 had been successful, as there were plans for them to share a new stadium that would have been purpose-built for the tournament. Despite all this neighbourliness, the rivalry between the two clubs is an extremely keen one.

— KAISER HAILS KINGS IN WAITING —

'England have so many talented young players, which means they will be a top team for many years to come. They will be contenders next summer [2002] and by the 2006 World Cup in Germany they could be the best team in the world.'

Franz Beckenbauer predicts a bright future for English football in 2001.

— LONGEST SERVING MANAGERS —

Manager	Club	Appointed
Dario Gradi	Crewe Alexandra	June 1983
Sir Alex Ferguson	Manchester United	November 1986
Alan Curbishley	Charlton Athletic	July 1991
Barry Fry	Peterborough United	August 1996
Arsene Wenger	Arsenal	September 1996
Brian Laws	Scunthorpe United	February 1997
Ronnie Moore	Rotherham United	May 1997
Stan Ternent	Burnley	June 1998
Gerard Houllier	Liverpool	November 1998
Sir Bobby Robson	Newcastle United	September 1999
Sam Allardyce	Bolton Wanderers	October 1999
Neil Warnock	Sheffield United	December 1999
Steve McMahon	Blackpool	January 2000
Gary Megson	West Bromwich Albion	March 2000
Graeme Souness	Blackburn Rovers	March 2000
Danny Wilson	Bristol City	June 2000
Andy Hessenthaler	Gillingham	June 2000
Sean O'Driscoll	Bournemouth	August 2000
Claudio Ranieri	Chelsea	September 2000

— THE GENTLE GIANT REMEMBERED —

There were plenty of famous British exports before David Beckham's departure for Real Madrid. Gary Lineker, Mark Hughes, Trevor Francis and Liam Brady are just a few from recent decades, but although each enjoyed varying degrees of success after leaving the rigours of the English game, none left such an indelible mark on Continental football as William John Charles, CBE. The finest footballer Wales has ever produced, he was the complete player, winning international renown as both a centre-forward and centre-half.

Born in Cwm-du, near Swansea, Charles joined the local ground staff at Swansea City as a youngster but was quickly spotted by Major Frank Buckley, the Leeds manager, and taken north (although his mother protested to the scout that he could not go to England because he did not have a passport!). After making his League debut aged 17 at centre-half, he became Wales's youngest capped player at 18 years and 71 days, and his goalscoring inspired Leeds to secure promotion in 1956 to the First Division. The following season he became the top-flight's leading marksman with 38 goals.

In 1957 he was transferred to Juventus for £65,000, a record for a British player, and the Welshman was an instant success. After his first game, an Italian newspaper carried the headline: 'Charles e Mezza Squadra' ('Charles Is Half A Team'), and he helped his new club go on to win the League title with 28 goals, winning the Italian League Player Of The Season award in the process. In his five seasons with the club, Juventus won three League titles and two Italian cups, and Charles himself scored 105 goals in 168 games.

Charles was released by Juventus for the 1958 World Cup, when Wales qualified for the finals of a major championship for the only time in history. However, he was heavily marked and was so savagely fouled in the victory over Hungary that he could not take part in the quarter-final, which Brazil won. He won a total of 38 caps, scoring 15 goals, although he frequently appeared in defence and during his spell at Juventus was often prevented from representing Wales.

Although Charles was 6'2" (1.88m) tall and weighed 14 stone (89kg), he seldom used his size and strength unnecessarily. He was never cautioned – let alone sent off – during his career, earning him the nickname 'The Gentle Giant' from his Italian fans. Once, in a game in Bologna, Charles was scythed down. He then proceeded to lecture his aggressor, who bowed his head while the referee looked on compliantly.

John Charles: born December 1931, died February 2004.

— FASTEST HAT-TRICK RECORDS —

Official World Record: 2 min 14 sec, James O'Connor, for Shelbourne against Bohemians, 1967

International: 3 min 15 sec, Masashi Nakayama, for Japan against Brunei, 2000

Premiership: 4 min 30 sec, Robbie Fowler, for Liverpool against Arsenal, 1994

Football League: 2 min 20 sec, James Hayter, for Bournemouth against Wrexham, 2004 (see page 82)

FA Cup: 2 min 20 sec, Andy Locke, for Nantwich Town against Droylesden, 1995

Scotland: 2 min 30 sec, Ian St John, for Motherwell against Hibernian, 1959

— A RECORD RUN —

Celtic's 5–1 victory over Livingston at Celtic Park on 29 February 2004 established a Scottish League record of 25 successive League victories in one season. It had been, at that point, ten months since Celtic had lost in the League. The last team before Celtic to establish a run of 25 successive League victories had been Morton, although their feat had been in the Second Division and had spanned two seasons, consisting of the final two matches of the 1962–63 season and the first 23 matches of the 1963–64 season.

— WOMEN'S FOOTBALL —

Women's football seems very much a 21st century sport. Yet the seed for female soccer was sown a long time ago; only male chauvinism prevented it from flourishing. Back in 1895 the British Ladies' Football Club was formed. When its members turned out for their first match at Crouch End – wearing shin guards, nightcaps and knee-length skirts – some 10,000 turned up to spectate. The football authorities of the era labelled it a farce.

In April 1920 England's women footballers played their first international against Scotland in front of a 25,000-strong crowd. The same year, Dick Kerr's Ladies proved they were the strongest women's team of the day by beating St Helen's 4–0. This all happened when women doing men's stuff – like football and voting – caused extreme disquiet.

The FA made its move in 1921 to support Britain's undermined male population. It banned women's football from being played at Football League grounds, saying, 'Complaints have been made as to football being played by women. The council feel impelled to express their strong opinion that the game of football is quite unsuitable for females so ought not to be encouraged.'

Those words sounded a death knell for women's football for decades. Similar suffocating prohibitions were issued in Holland, Germany and, bizarrely, during the Qing dynasty in China. It wasn't until 1971 that the ludicrous ban was repealed in England, two years after organised women's football began taking place again. In 1972 England's women played their first officially endorsed international, but still football remained male-dominated with women players battling all manner of prejudice and slurs. It was the same story off the pitch.

The first woman to win the job of general manager of a football team in the English League was Annie Bassett who took up her post with Reading in 1988.

A year later Ron Atkinson said, 'Women should be in the kitchen, the discotheque and the boutique, but not in football.'

Despite the dinosaurs, the present Women's Football League was established in 1991 in England. Worldwide the sport was heading for the stratosphere. By 1999 the American winners of the Women's World Cup – which was played before capacity crowds – became household names. Although women's soccer in England has failed to match the success of teams across the Atlantic, the FA had the satisfaction of announcing that by 2002 football had become the top sport of choice among women and girls.

— FANTASTIC FAN —

When it comes to Manchester United, there are few more devoted fans than Ray Adler. And season-ticket holder Ray continues his passion when he leaves the pitch-side by collecting Manchester United memorabilia. It all began with programmes. Ray saw some old copies for sale and snapped them up. Before too long he possessed every programme printed since 1944.

Then he turned his attention to other items, including tickets, photos – and even menus. 'After European games, teams normally fly straight home these days, but back in the 1960s, when it was more difficult to travel, clubs often hosted official dinners after the match. United held many of theirs at the Midland Hotel, a particular favourite of Matt Busby's.'

His considerable collection has cost him dear. He reckons that he has parted with more than £150,000 while gathering it together. Some items are kept at his home but the most valuable are stored securely in a bank's vault. Perhaps the three most significant pieces, worth £15,000 apiece, are a 1902 brochure printed when Manchester United were known as Newton Heath, a 1968 programme from the World Club Championship in Argentina when United were beaten by Estudiantes and a programme from the same year from Sarajevo printed during United's successful European Cup run.

— TEN LOW SPOTS IN ENGLISH FOOTBALL —

1923: Huge crowds stampede at Wembley before, during and after the first ever FA Cup final to be staged at the new stadium, between Bolton Wanderers and West Ham. Hundreds are injured.

1968: Alan Mullery becomes the first England player to be sent off during a full international. Mullery was dispatched after kicking a Yugoslavian opponent who had felled him with a late tackle.

1971: Rioting Leeds fans win the support of the club manager and chairman. 'I don't blame them at all. The referee's decision in allowing West Bromwich's second goal was diabolical,' said Don Revie. 'I am not blaming the spectators. There was every justification for it,' Alderman Percy Woodward, the club's chairman, declared.

1974: Billy Bremner and Kevin Keegan are the first Football League players to be sent off at Wembley during that year's Charity Shield. (The first player sent off at Wembley was an Argentinian, Rattin, during the 1966 World Cup.)

1985: More than 50 fans die as fire sweeps through the main stand at Bradford City's ground during a match against Lincoln.

1985: More than 40 people are killed after a safety fence collapses at Heysel Stadium following an onslaught from rioting Liverpool and Juventus fans.

1989: Ninety-four soccer fans are crushed to death at Hillsborough during the FA Cup semi-final between Liverpool and Nottingham Forest.

1995: Eric Cantona executes a kung-fu-style kick on a Crystal Palace fan.

1999: Robbie Fowler celebrates a goal by sniffing the touch line as if it were a line of cocaine.

2004: Three Leicester City players are held after a mid-season training break in Spain ends in allegations of sexual misconduct.

— GOAL FEST —

Everyone likes to see his or her team mount a valiant comeback in a match that seemed doomed to end in defeat. What a treat was in store, then, for Charlton fans when their team was trailing at the Valley ground against Huddersfield on 21 December 1957. First Charlton had gone down to ten men after centre-half Derek Ufton broke his collarbone. By half time Charlton were 2–0 behind and within ten minutes of the start of the second half the score was a galling 5–1 to Huddersfield. But Charlton players were nothing if not ambitious that afternoon, particularly so left-footed winger Johnny Summers who used his weaker right foot to slam home five goals in swift succession. Huddersfield snatched back an equaliser with just two minutes on the clock. However, Summers wasn't finished either and he set up centre-forward Johnny Ryan for the seventh goal scored with the last kick of the game. Final result, Charlton 7, Huddersfield 6.

— NO CONTEST —

With Celtic light years ahead in the SPL, the 2003–04 season run-in was dominated by scathing talk of the Scottish Procession League. However – at least from a spurious mathematical perspective – SPL clubs have slightly more chance of title honours than the sassenach elite south of the border. Here's the dodgy logic.

Most people agree that only two clubs are ever serious contenders for the SPL: Rangers and Celtic. With a total of 12 clubs in the League, this means that 16.66 per cent of the League's membership has a reasonable expectation of success. In the Premiership – let's face it – its generally down to Arsenal and Manchester United. Chelsea have shown us the money, but not necessarily the bottle. Liverpool and Newcastle are currently not good/rich enough to be serious players. So if we do the sums as above we find that just 10 per cent of the 20 Premiership sides have a reasonable prospect of glory. Therefore, go North for more excitement. Simple, innit?

— THE AMATEURS' HOUR —

Queen's Park are Scotland's oldest club and the only club in the senior Scottish and English Leagues whose players are entirely amateur. They are also the only Scottish club to have reached the FA Cup final, losing 2–1 to Blackburn Rovers at the Kennington Oval in 1884 and by 2–0 to the same opponents at the same venue in 1885. Queen's Park had played in Football Association competitions following their formation in 1867 because there was, at that time, no Scottish Football Association in existence. Following the formation of the SFA in 1873, Queen's Park played in both the English and Scottish Cup competitions and won the SFA's newly inaugurated Scottish Cup eight times in its first 13 seasons and then twice more in the 1890s.

The recognition of professionalism in Scottish football in 1893 and the decision of the Queen's Park committee to remain amateur signalled the end of their domination of Scottish football. Their special status as the first great Scottish club is reflected in their being landlords of Hampden Park, Scotland's national stadium, which Queen's Park opened in 1903, and which the club leases to the SFA. The current lease stretches over 20 years at a cost to the SFA of £800,000 per annum, allowing the Queen's Park board to maintain the stadium and spend approximately £150,000 a year on developing young players, all amateur, and fulfilling their motto of *Ludere causa ludendi*: 'The game for the game's sake'.

— HOW DID THEY DO THAT? —

Let's not get weighed down with the unacceptable face of English football. Let's focus instead on the great moments in the history of the English game. Well, it's just one moment actually and that's when England won the World Cup (aka the Jules Rimet Trophy) in 1966. How did they do it? In addition to the four goals, there were a further 41 attempts at goal by England. One hit the post, ten were saved, six were blocked and three deflected, while 21 were wide or high. That compares with West Germany's 37 attempts at goal, two of which were successful. England also won six corners and 36 throw-ins and took 16 goal kicks compared with the German side's 12 corners, 19 throw-ins and 24 goal kicks. England came through the group stages following a goalless draw with Uruguay and 2–0 victories over Mexico and France. In the quarter-final England beat Argentina 1–0 and in the semi-final the team ousted Portugal with a 2–1 scoreline. The referee was Gottfried Dienst, from Switzerland, while linesmen Galba and Bakhramov came from Czechoslovakia and the USSR respectively. During the ensuing victory parade the crowd sang 'When The Saints Go Marching In'.

— WALKING AWAY —

'If one day I should return to soccer, it would mean it has changed. I've been through the system. I left it because it was no longer similar to my vision of the game. Because of all the financial interests at stake, the sport is turning into a mafia.'

Eric Cantona (the Premiership's original superstar), February 2001

— NO HALF-MEASURES —

Watford's 5–4 interval lead away to Burnley on 5 April 2003 constituted the highest-scoring first half in the League in 67 years. The only other League nine-goal first half came on December 1935 when Tranmere Rovers led Oldham Athletic 8–1 at home on their way to a 13–4 win. The English record is Tottenham Hotspur 10, Crewe Alexandra 0 in the FA Cup in 1960 (the result was 13–2), while a more recent first-half goal rush in the UEFA Cup occurred in September 1976 when Derby County beat Finn Harps 12–0 at home, having been 9–0 ahead at the break.

— THE MANY CLUBS OF JOHN BURRIDGE —

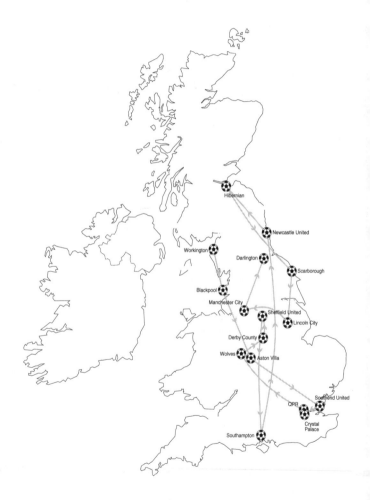

— DROPPING LIKE STONES —

Clubs promoted from the Conference have a right to feel optimistic, but the fate of Maidstone United, nicknamed the Stones, should provide a salutary lesson for all those directors who are dreaming of European football while their team plays Southend United on a wet Wednesday night. Founded in 1897 as successors to Maidstone Invicta, United had spent much of their long history as an amateur outfit, the club's most notable success arriving in 1979 when they battled through to the third round of the FA Cup.

Understandable jubilation greeted their Conference victory of 1989, which brought League football to Dartford for the first time. Early results produced a record victory of 6–1 against Scunthorpe United, and the little Kent club continued to defy their critics by only narrowly missing promotion to the old Third Division at the first attempt.

It all came to an end, however, in 1992, when the club was overcome by a financial crisis and lack of a home ground. A bizarre last-minute attempt to save their League status by moving lock, stock and barrel 320 miles (515km) north to Tyneside proved unacceptable to supporters and the club went out of existence before reforming, once more, as Maidstone Invicta.

A SELECTION OF FOOTBALLERS WHO HAVE PLAYED IN — EACH OF THE PREMIERSHIP, SERIE A AND LA LIGA —

Laurent Blanc	Manchester Utd, Inter Milan, Barcelona
Winston Bogarde	Chelsea, AC Milan, Barcelona
Didier Deschamps	Chelsea, Juventus, Valencia
Paulo Futre	West Ham, AC Milan, Atletico Madrid
Christian Karembeu	Middlesbrough, Sampdoria, Real Madrid
Darko Kovacevic	Sheffield Wednesday, Juventus, Real Sociedad
Savo Milosevic	Aston Villa, Juventus, Real Sociedad
Christian Panucci	Chelsea, AC Milan, Real Madrid

A SELECTION OF FOOTBALLERS WHO HAVE PLAYED IN EACH OF THE PREMIERSHIP, SERIE A AND LA LIGA
— (CONT'D) —

Gica Popescu	Spurs, Lecce, Barcelona
Florin Raducioiu	West Ham, AC Milan, Espanyol
Stefan Schwarz	Arsenal, Fiorentina, Valencia
Mario Stanic	Chelsea, Parma, Sporting Gijon
Nelson Vivas	Arsenal, Inter, Celta Vigo

— BUSBY BABES —

English football has always been characterised by tremendous highs and terrible lows, and no one knew this better than the legendary Manchester United manager Sir Matt Busby. He saw his promising team decimated by one of sport's worst-ever tragedies and was himself left at death's door. Then he recovered to bring glory to club and country.

As a young man he played for Manchester City and Liverpool. But the cup finals he played in and the international caps he accrued seem tame compared to what lay ahead.

He became the post-war manager of Manchester United and built up an FA Cup- and League-winning side under the captaincy of Johnny Carey, in 1948 and 1952 respectively. As the team aged Busby introduced fresh blood, and it was these players who were tipped for triumph in the European Cup.

They were returning from Belgrade where they had drawn 3–3 with Red Star to win a place in the semi-finals in February 1958. The aircraft they were in crashed on take-off at a snow-covered Munich airport, where it had stopped to refuel. Two attempts to get airborne had already been aborted. After the third failed, the plane ploughed through the perimeter fence at the end of the runway. Before coming to a halt the craft had split in half and one wing had smashed into a house.

Aboard were the Manchester United football team, club officials and match journalists. Among the dead were captain Roger Byrne, 28; Geoff Bent, 25; Eddie Colman, 21; Mark Jones, 24; David Pegg, 22; Tommy Taylor, 26; and Liam 'Billy' Whelan, 22. The highly rated Duncan Edwards, 21, died later. Taylor, Pegg and Byrne were all England players, while Whelan represented the Republic Of Ireland.

Club secretary Walter Crickmer, coach Bert Whalley and trainer Tom Curry were also killed along with eight sports writers, including Frank Swift, the former England 'keeper (see page 19). Survivors included Busby, who was in a critical condition after his chest was crushed. Shortly after the crash a doctor said, 'He has little chance. His condition is worsening.' Bobby Charlton, Dennis Viollet and Jackie Blanchflower were among those players to escape with their lives but were left deeply shocked.

Busby fought his personal battle first, finally winning his way back to full health. Then he turned his attentions back to United, ready once again to build up a Championship team. Typically, he was prepared to invest time, energy and money in the task.

To illustrate their commitment, Manchester United players wore a special shirt depicting a phoenix rising from the ashes in the 1958 FA Cup final.

In May 1968 the rebuilt team rewarded Busby's faith and patience by bringing home the European Cup after beating Benfica at Wembley 4–1. Bobby Charlton scored twice – once with a header – while George Best and Brian Kidd got one apiece. Busby was further rewarded with a knighthood.

The following year, Sir Matt announced that he was giving up his job as team manager to become United's general manager. With this declaration the League's longest-serving manager stepped down. That season, Manchester United added not a scrap of silverware to the cabinet at Old Trafford. He went on to become president of the club. Sir Matt died in 1994, following a long illness.

— THE £4,000 PENALTY —

FA rules state that players are not supposed to bet on any game other than through the football pools. However, Graham Sharpe of UK bookmakers William Hill has confirmed that certain unidentified players take advantage of inside knowledge. 'We see it as legitimate gamesmanship,' he said. 'If a team changes their penalty taker and we don't know about it then they may be getting 25–1 or 33–1 about what is really a 10–1 shot.'

Graham was no doubt recalling the famous 1992 incident in which Colchester United's squad pulled off an entirely legal betting coup. They backed defender Martin Granger as United's first scorer in a Cup match against Northampton Town. The bookies offered 20–1, about right for a back-four player.

However, the Colchester lads knew that Granger had just been made penalty taker by player-manager Roy McDonough, the usual spot-kick specialist. Sure enough, Colchester got a penalty, Granger belted it home and his team-mates celebrated a collective win of £4,000. It made the 2–1 defeat a bit easier to swallow.

— SMALL TOWN STADIA —

The English League club hailing from the smallest town appears to be Rushden And Diamonds, whose Nene Park ground can be found in Irthlingborough, Northamptonshire, (population 6,000). Also in the frame is Port Vale, which, although not representative of anywhere in particular, happens to have a ground in Burslem (population 20,600), Staffs.

Turning this trivia snippet on its head, it's worth noting the largest towns that have (so far) had to manage without League football. Front-runners here include Dudley (population 310,000), Salford (216,000), Warrington (191,000) and Basingstoke (152,000). Of course, it doesn't mean the townsfolk of these boroughs have to go without a Premiership fix. Most likely, they're all card-carrying members of the Manchester United supporters' club. Anyway, they could always move to Milton Keynes and watch Wimbledon.

— FOOTBALL PITCH MARKINGS —

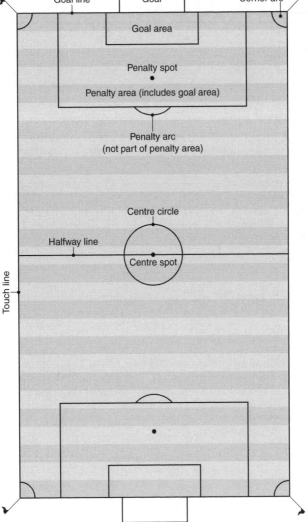

— SICKIE STATS —

Darren Anderton and Jamie Redknapp are constantly pilloried by fans for being injury-prone. Yet there are a handful of other stars (all right, at least three) who out-sicknote them in an English crocks league, led by former Sheffield Wednesday and Scotland international Phil O'Donnell.

And before you ask, we haven't forgotten Michael Bridges whose APS (Appearances Per Season) averages out at a pitiful 16.6. Fair play to the lad, he'd only been around six seasons when this handy primer up to and including the 2002–03 campaign was put together.

PLAYER	NO OF APPS (CLUB AND COUNTRY) (INC AS SUB)	NO OF SEASONS	AVERAGE APPS PER SEASON
Phil O'Donnell	248	13	19.07
Darren Eadie	223	10	22.3
Duncan Ferguson	256	10	25.6
Jamie Redknapp	300	10	30.0
Darren Anderton	379	10	37.9

— SOCCER TIPS —

In August 1997 one of the football world's most sensational criminal trials laid bare the murky world of international sports bookmaking. The crux of the allegation was that Liverpool's eccentric goalkeeper Bruce Grobbelaar had taken cash payments of up to £40,000 to fix certain Premiership matches. The case, which followed an investigation by *The Sun* newspaper, ended when Grobbelaar and fellow pros John Fashanu and Hans Segers were all cleared of a conspiracy to throw games. A fourth defendant, Malaysian entrepreneur Heng Suan Lim, was also acquitted.

It had been the men's second trial on charges linked to a Malaysian betting syndicate which, according to the prosecution, made complex wagers on winning margins and score aggregates in the Premiership. Six months earlier a jury had failed to reach a verdict.

One of the games under suspicion was Newcastle United's 3–0 victory over Liverpool in November 1993. Grobbelaar had supposedly fixed the result at that score, and Winchester Crown Court was treated to the glorious spectacle of former Scotland 'keeper Bob Wilson and England legend Gordon Banks giving expert views on whether Grobbelaar deliberately fluffed his attempted saves. They concluded there was no evidence that any defendant had thrown a game.

Sadly for soccer, it didn't end here. Grobbelaar sued *The Sun* for libel and won £85,000 damages. The newspaper appealed, the Court of Appeal overturned the libel jury's verdict as 'perverse' and awarded full costs of £1.2 million against Grobbelaar. He then appealed to the UK's highest court, the House of Lords, which by a 4–1 majority reinstated the verdict but cut the costs award to a nominal £1 – leaving Bruce massively in debt.

The senior judge, Lord Bingham, was acidly clear about the goalkeeper's conduct: 'It would be an affront to justice', he said, 'if a court of law were to award substantial damages to a man shown to have acted in such flagrant breach of his legal and moral obligations.'

Predictably, underground betting syndicates in Malaysia, Thailand and Indonesia came under the microscope amid claims that they were behind a £350 million worldwide 'bung' industry. One leading Malaysian sports writer, Johnson Fernandez of *The Malay Mail*, revealed that bookmakers budgeted up to £25,000 to fix a result: 'The usual *modus operandi*', he claimed, 'is to approach one player, often the goalkeeper, and leave him to sort everything out with his team-mates.'

Fernandez insisted that several high-profile British players had been bribed (though he didn't identify them) and quoted specific games between Liverpool and QPR, Arsenal and Sheffield Wednesday, and Aston Villa and Manchester United in which match-fixing had been attempted.

— THE FORECAST IS...REALLY LOUSY —

In the good old days when watching football meant Bovril, beer fumes, stale pies and smokers' cough, just about everyone did the pools. There were various mind-numbingly complicated plans in which weirdly nicknamed punters tipped mystifying 'perms', but essentially the idea was – and is – to predict eight score draws from the English and Scottish Saturday fixture list, so scooping a big-money jackpot.

Although the pools companies have always been quick to publicise big winners (not that anyone much cares these days) they've been a little less forthcoming about the true odds. Suffice it to say, there are 2 billion sets of eight matches which can be permed from a pool of 58.

As for the idea that analytical ability and football knowledge plays its part, er, no. In the early 1990s a researcher slipped on his anorak and analysed the predictions of three 'professional' newspaper pools pundits. He established that when they unanimously tipped a score draw, their actual success in those games was a heady 5 per cent. Best off, shut your eyes and stick a pin in your coupon.

The popularity of the Lottery during the 1990s all but destroyed the pools business. Total stakes plummeted by 60 per cent between 1993 and 1999 to the point where just 8 per cent of UK adults admitted to being regular players. Despite this, Littlewoods forked out £1.35 million to take over rivals Zetters in August 2002, bolstering its punter base by 60,000, to well over 2 million. That's 85 per cent of the total UK market.

— SEEING RED —

Pace isn't the only aspect of the game to have increased in the last couple of decades. Bookings and sendings-off have proliferated to the point that the days when all was forgotten over a handshake and a pint in the club bar are but a rose-tinted memory. The result? All major disciplinary records have been set since 1982.

MOST RED CARDS IN A SEASON

371 (League alone) 1998–99

MOST RED CARDS IN A DAY

15 (all League).......................................31 October 1998
15 (3 League, 12 FA Cup*) ....20 November 1982
26 (14 English, 12 Scottish) ....16 October 1999

MOST RED CARDS IN A WEEKEND

15 (League alone).......................................22–23 December 1990

FIRST RED CARD IN AN FA CUP FINAL

Kevin Moran, Manchester United v Everton 1985

QUICKEST RED CARD

Walter Boyd, Swansea City ....23 November 1999
   v Darlington, Third Division
   (As substitute in zero seconds)

MOST RED CARDS IN ONE GAME

5: Chesterfield (2) v Plymouth Argyle (3) ....22 February 1997
5: Wigan Athletic (1) v Bristol Rovers (4) ....2 December 1997
5: Exeter City (3) v Cambridge United (2) ....23 November 2002

MOST RED CARDS GIVEN TO ONE TEAM

Wigan Athletic (1) v Bristol Rovers (4)...................2 December 1997
Hereford United (4) v Northampton Town (0)....11 November 1992

*Worst overall FA Cup total

— LAST-GASP GLORY —

They are one of the greatest – or most heartbreaking – aspects of football, those last-gasp, final-minute shots from nowhere that either rescue a team's ambitions or destroy those of another. The ten greatest, in descending order:

England 2 Greece 2

2 October 2001: David Beckham sent England into the World Cup finals with a free-kick at Old Trafford.

— LAST-GASP GLORY (CONT'D) —

Paris Saint-Germain 2 Bordeaux 3
29 May 1999: Pascal Feindouno, an 18-year-old triallist, came on to pip Marseille to the title.

Arsenal 3 Manchester United 2
12 May 1979: United had scored twice in the previous three minutes but Alan Sunderland won the FA Cup with his strike.

France 2 Italy 1
2 July 2000: Sylvain Wiltord equalised for France deep into injury time, before they went on to win the European Championship.

Blackpool 4 Bolton Wanderers 3
2 May 1953: Stanley Matthews crossed for Bill Perry to score the FA Cup-winning goal.

Charlton Athletic 7 Huddersfield Town 6
21 December 1957: Ten-man Charlton trailed 5–1 with half an hour left, but John Ryan won them the match with the last kick.

England 4 West Germany 2
30 July 1966: Geoff Hurst completed his hat-trick to confirm England's only World Cup win.

Carlisle United 2 Plymouth Argyle 1
8 May 1999: A goal in the 95th minute, from Carlisle United goalkeeper Jimmy Glass, kept them in the Football League.

Manchester United 2 Bayern Munich 1
26 May 1999: Ole Gunnar Solskjaer volleyed the European Cup-winning goal after United trailed going into injury time.

Liverpool 0 Arsenal 2
26 May 1989: Michael Thomas scored for Arsenal nine seconds from the end of the season, beating Liverpool, the only team that could have finished above them, to the Championship.

— THE END OF THE WORLD —

'It won't be the end of the world, but it will be close to that.'

Manchester City manager Malcolm Allison with some prophetic words ahead of his team's shock defeat to Halifax Town in the FA Cup, 1980.

— SHOOTING SPECTACULAR —

The penalty shoot-out has always had its detractors. For some, the only way to achieve a definitive result in a game is to continue playing football until someone scores. The penalty shoot-out, they argue, is too much like a lottery. Aberdeen manager Alex Smith went further in 1990 when his team won the Tennents Scottish Cup after the match against Celtic remained goalless for 120 minutes. It was the first year that replays had been ruled out in the Cup competition. 'Penalty shoot-outs have nothing to do with football,' Smith declared. 'It's like shooting poor wee ducks at a fairground.'

Maybe, but some penalty shoot-outs are thrilling affairs. Take a 1996 encounter in the Turkish domestic cup competition between Genclerbirligi and Galatasaray, which ended 17–16 to Genclerbirligi. Even that has been exceeded, though, in Argentina in 1988 where drawn matches in the championship automatically went to penalties. The two teams were Argentinos Juniors and Racing Club. The score was ultimately 20–19 to Argentinos. The players and the spectators were left exhausted by tension.

The sad fact is that penalty shoot-outs provide drama and spectacle at the end of what is sometimes a dire match. Word has it that the afore mentioned 1990 Scottish Cup final would have been a wash-out except for the penalties at the end when the crowd saw no fewer than 17 goals hit the back of the net.

— ONE AND ONLY —

The only footballer to win an international cap among the ranks of registered Hartlepool United players was Ambrose Fogarty, who played for the Republic Of Ireland in 1964. Fogarty began his career at Hartlepool in 1963 following a £10,000 transfer from Sunderland, a club record.

— LEAGUE CHAMPIONS —

Who's won and how often...

— TEN TREBLE FACTS —

1. Manchester United scored a total of 128 goals in the 1998–99 season.

2. Peter Schmeichel captained the side during the match against Bayern Munich as the usual incumbent, Roy Keane, was suspended.

3. On the night United won the treble, Sir Matt Busby would have been celebrating his 90th birthday if he had lived.

4. Bayern Munich colours were already tied to the European Club Champions Cup when United scored – twice.

5. United lost only three matches in the domestic League, against Middlesbrough, Arsenal and Sheffield Wednesday.

6. In the Premier League the Reds conceded an average of 0.97 goals per game.

7. Top goalscorer that season was Dwight Yorke, who netted 29. In second place was Andy Cole with 24 and third came Ole Gunnar Solskjaer with 18.

8. David Beckham and Dwight Yorke gave the greatest number of assists that season, each presenting their team-mates with 23 goal-scoring opportunities.

9. Of the treble-winning squad two players, Wes Brown and Nicky Butt, were born in Manchester. Paul Scholes was born in nearby Salford.

10. Teddy Sheringham scored the first goal for Manchester United in their 2–0 victory over Newcastle in the FA Cup final just 90 seconds after replacing the injured Roy Keane.

— A JOKE —

For those of you who loathe to be reminded of United's glorious moment...

Q: 'How many Manchester United fans does it take to change a lightbulb?'

A: 'Two. One to change it and the other to drive her up from London.'

— PLEASE MISTER, CAN WE HAVE OUR BALLS BACK? —

It sounds Pythonesque, but with the 2003–04 season barely three months old, North Devon Sunday League outfit Appledore FC revealed it was suing its neighbour Paul Vose for refusing to return £800 worth of stray balls. Just to be clear, this was the combined value of the 18 which had sailed over one goal and into Mr Vose's garden.

The club claimed it was being financially crippled and complained that an agreement in which committee members had been allowed to recover balls after games had collapsed. An attempt to get Mr Vose prosecuted for theft failed when he promised police he'd return the lot at the end of the season.

Club chairman Larry Jones, who runs a fish and chip shop in nearby Bideford, said, 'It's a crazy situation. We have tried to be neighbourly but Mr Vose isn't interested.

'We've had our ground for over a century. He moved in two years ago. Why live next to a football pitch if you're worried by stray balls?

'Mr Vose says we should shoot on target. But if David Beckham can put one miles over the bar for England occasionally, surely our lads can be forgiven. We can't take these losses anymore. Our players only get paid if they win – and their match fee wouldn't buy more than a few beers.'

The club's lawyers reckoned it was unreasonable to confiscate the balls and warned Mr Vose that if he didn't keep them pumped up the leather would deteriorate, leading to a possible action for criminal damage. It wasn't as though, they pleaded, the club had ignored its responsibility to protect his garden. Indeed, there was 30ft-high netting behind the offending goal during matches. Sadly, this saved only a handful of balls from garden purgatory.

Mr Vose, a 56-year-old Manchester City supporter who runs a printing business in Bideford, locked the footballs in his shed. 'I've no problem with the balls,' he said, 'it's the players I object to. I used to play Sunday League myself and

I know that shots go astray. But when players break through your hedge, knock down your fence and start shouting obscenities at you it's time to hit back.

'The police have been round telling me this and that but I know my rights. I asked the bobby if he'd mind me coming round his place with half a dozen mates at the weekend so that we can kick footballs into his garden and shout abuse. The club can sue if it wants. The balls may be in my garden but the ball's in their court.'

— TOSH VERSUS THE GODFATHER —

Every manager knows it can be hard to quit a club when the fans like you. However, not as hard as much-travelled coach John Toshack found it when he tried to leave Sicilian side Catania in Serie B of the Italian League.

On 28 January 2003 Tosh handed in his resignation following a row over team selection with Catania's youthful president. The following evening he was woken at midnight in his hotel room by a man looking not entirely dissimilar to Marlon Brando in *The Godfather*. Marlon apparently had 'businesses' in Miami and had agreed to lead a delegation of 'supporters' – that's right, the 25 men waiting outside – to persuade Tosh to stay on.

John explained his mind was made up. Marlon explained that he and his friends outside *liked* John. He didn't need to explain that they might not like him if he left Catania. John pointed out that it was too late. He'd signed his release documents and the club had already posted them to the Italian Federation in Rome. 'What,' said Marlon, producing a sheaf of papers, 'you mean these documents?'

Tosh did manage to walk away from Catania. But he made sure his next job was in Spain.

— CURSE OF THE METATARSAL —

Remember the agony of England fans during the run-up to the 2002 World Cup? Both David Beckham and Danny Murphy broke second metatarsal bones, and because, like No 10 buses, these things always come along in threes, Gary Neville did his fifth metatarsal just before the tournament began.

The metatarsals are 3in (7.6cm) long bones which help share the load of your weight and adjust easily to uneven ground. They tend to be broken by having heavy objects dropped on them (like a defender's foot) or by twisting when your foot position remains fixed.

The real key to knowing your metatarsals from your navicular – and therefore being feted as a sports-injury expert by your pals – is to memorise this diagram and wait for a bad tackle on your star winger. Then, look thoughtful, shake your head and say something like, 'Could be a meta. He'll need RICE for that.' When your mystified companion queries the healing benefits of a Chinese meal, simply look scornful and reply, 'Rest, Ice, Compression and Elevation, dummy.'

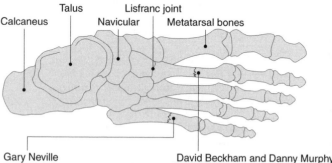

Calcaneus   Talus   Lisfranc joint   Navicular   Metatarsal bones

Gary Neville
broke his fifth metatarsal
ahead of the tournament in 2002

David Beckham and Danny Murphy
both broke second metatarsal bone
in the run-up to World Cup 2002

— WINNERS IN WOLVES CLOTHING —

Wolverhampton have wandered all over the League divisions – and their trips up and down the tables have not been without reward. The club became the first to win all the divisions during its chequered history. It peaked in the '50s, winning the Division One title in 1954, 1958 and 1959. This was when the side was captained by the inimitable centre-half Billy Wright, who became the world's first player to win 100 caps when he led England to victory over Scotland in 1959. Prior to this glorious era Wolves were in the Second Division and won it in 1932 (as they did again in 1977). The Fourth Division was secured by Wolves in 1988 and the following season players pocketed the Third Division. If that wasn't enough Wolves have even won the Third Division North (in the distant 1923–24 season) when England's clubs observed the North–South divide.

Honour also is due to Burnley, who conquered the First Division twice: in 1921 and 1960. The Second Division title came their way in 1973, as well as 1898, while the Third Division was claimed in 1982. The title that completed the set, that of the Fourth Division, was clinched in 1992.

Other teams have also nearly accomplished the feat. Nottingham Forest, Derby County, Huddersfield Town and Blackburn Rovers have won three out of the four titles but that oh-so-important fourth has so far eluded them.

Thanks to swift progress through the tables, Wimbledon have a handful of players who wore club colours in Divisions 4, 3, 2 and 1 between 1982 and 1987. Three of them, Alan Cork, Kevin Gage and Glyn Hodges, also scored in each of the divisions.

— PIRES ON WENGER —

'His pre-match talk lasts seven minutes – any longer and he reckons it would be counter-productive… it's all very compressed and to the point. For him, football has to be a game everyone can understand.'

Robert Pires explains Arsène Wenger's philosophy on pre-match pep talks in his autobiography, Robert Pires Footballeur.

— THEATRE OF DREAMS —

It was thought to be an impossible dream. Until 1999, winning the Premiership and the FA Cup in the same season was believed to be the pinnacle of English footballing achievement. Alex Ferguson had different ideas and he propelled his side into the record books when Manchester United secured the European Clubs Champions Cup on 26 May at the Nou Camp stadium in Barcelona.

It was a story of derring-do, never-say-die and a score of other clichés. None of the results from the crucial matches were predictable, and the soccer-loving public in general and United fans in particular were kept on the edge of their seats throughout.

United pinched the Premiership by beating Spurs at Old Trafford 2–1. The team had, however, gone behind in the first half to a Les Ferdinand goal that resulted in distant Arsenal fans singing (perhaps for the first time): 'Come on, you Spurs.' Arsenal had stumbled in two out of the last three of their matches that season and needed United to lose in order to claim the title. United didn't and it was the fifth time in seven seasons that the trophy had gone back to Old Trafford.

The FA Cup run was most memorable for two clashes with Arsenal. The first was goalless and the second was locked at 1–1 when Arsenal were awarded a penalty. A place in the final seemed assured until 'keeper Peter Schmeichel stretched his mighty frame to save Dennis Bergkamp's shot. In extra time, Ryan Giggs took the ball around five Arsenal players to score what has been dubbed one of the most brilliant solo goals ever. Beating Newcastle in the final seemed tame by comparison.

When it came to playing Bayern Munich, it seemed German efficiency on the pitch would see off United, their undeniable flair and fight simply unable to produce results on the night. United had gone a goal down in the first six minutes of the game and the scoreline looked as if it would stay until a goal-mouth scuffle resulted in an equaliser from

Teddy Sheringham. Moments later in injury time Solskjaer netted the winner, sparking delirious elation among the ranks of United supporters and despair for those of Bayern. Both Sheringham and Solskjaer were brought on late in the game as substitutes. The result still seemed like a dream. United's tendency to leave the essential matter of winning to the final moments of the most crucial games gave the proud achievement a fairytale quality. It remains to be seen if any other team can match the Reds. It is unlikely anyone else could do so in such a spell-binding way.

— SPORTING CHANCES —

Footballers' wages have paved the way to lavish lifestyles and extraordinary excesses. Gambling is frequently a spin-off to this 'money-no-object' culture and there are numerous players who like a bet at the casino or on the gee-gees. Here's a list of ten soccer stars known to have a penchant for gambling:

1. Eidur Gudjohnsen
2. Jesper Gronkjaer
3. Jimmy Floyd Hasselbaink
4. Kieron Dyer
5. Paul Gascoigne
6. Paul Merson
7. Michael Owen
8. Keith Gillespie
9. Steve McManaman
10. Robbie Fowler

— BACKWARDS THINKING —

Imagine the delight of the soccer anoraks when Liverpool youth team player Leon Noel came to prominence. His name is the same spelled forwards or backwards – in other words, it's a palindrome. Worryingly, some soccer observers devote their lives to spotting satisfying oddities such as this...

— FOOTBALL FANZINES —

The terraces were once known as a home of original humour.
All right, some of it was lewd and a few chants displayed
some distinctly ropey rhymes. But it proved what a nimble-
minded bunch most football fans were. Now football
supporters can be creative and quick-witted away from the
ground through the pages of club fanzines. A fanzine is
made by the fans, for the fans. It is an independent forum
(although expect some bias towards its associated team) for
news and views, often labelled 'the people's programme'.
Since the advent of the internet, on-line fanzines have
mushroomed and evolved. Rather than delve into the pages
of individual fanzines it's probably sufficient here to provide
the frequently inexplicable titles of some fanzines past and
present and let your imagination do the rest . . .

- *Brian Moore's Head Looks Uncannily Like The London Planetarium* – Gillingham

- *Only Sing When We're Fishing* – Grimsby

- *Bert Trautmann's Helmet* – Manchester City

- *Knees Up Mother Brown* – West Ham

- *Grorty Dick* – West Bromwich Albion

- *Bob Lord's Sausage* – Burnley

- *Shiny Red Balls* – Nottingham Forest

- *Who's That Jumping Off The Pier?* – Preston North End

- *Hob Nob Anybody?* – Reading

- *Blind, Stupid And Desperate* – Watford

- *A Good Swedish Site* – Colchester

- *4,000 Holes* – Blackburn Rovers

- *Fly Me To The Moon* – Middlesbrough

- *Tripe N Trotters* – Bolton

— MINI SOCCER —

Mini soccer was introduced by the FA in September 2003 in the hope of encouraging more young players into the game.

According to FA guidelines, soccer players aged under seven and eight should play on a pitch that is no wider than 30 yards (27.45m) and no narrower than 20 yards (18.30m). Pitch length should lie between 30 yards (27.45m) and 50 yards (45.75m). Those aged under nine and ten should play on a pitch no wider than 40 yards (36.60m) and no narrower than 30 yards (27.45m). In length the pitch should be at least 50 yards (45.75m) but no longer than 60 yards (54.90m). The pitch should be bisected by a halfway line with the centre mark at its midway point. The penalty area is 10 yards (9.15m) deep and 19 yards (16.47m) long with a penalty mark 8 yards (7.32m) from the goal line in the centre of goal. Goal posts should stand 12 feet (3.6m) apart, with a crossbar at 6 feet (1.88m). For players aged eight and under a size three ball is recommended. Those aged under ten should use a size four ball.

Those children aged over six and under eight should play no more than ten minutes in each half of their game and no more than 45 minutes of football per day. Anyone aged over eight and under ten should play matches of two 15-minute halves and should not exceed an hour of football a day. Shin guards are compulsory.

— BIG JUMP —

Among players picked for the Turks and Caicos Islands to contest the World Cup 2006 qualifiers was central defender Lawrence Harvey. Lawrence, a 30-year-old quantity surveyor who plays most of his football for Sunday soccer side Aicia Athletic in the Halls Of Cambridge Senior League, qualified for selection because he'd worked on the islands for a couple of years. He isn't building up his hopes for Germany though. At the time of his call-up the Turks and Caicos team was placed 203rd out of 204 in FIFA's world rankings.

— TRANSFER RECORDS INVOLVING ENGLISH CLUBS—

£ Million

| 0 | 5 | 10 | 15 | 20 | 25 | 30 |

Rio Ferdinand Leeds United — Manchester United £29.1m 2002

Juan Veron Lazio — Manchester United £28.1m 2001

David Beckham Manchester United —
Real Madrid £25m 2003

Nicolas Anelka Arsenal — Real Madrid £23.5m 1999

Marc Overmars Arsenal — Barcelona £21.6m 2000

Ruud van Nistelrooy PSV — Manchester United
£19m 2001

Rio Ferdinand West Ham United —
Leeds United £18m 2000

Damien Duff Blackburn Rovers — Chelsea
£17m 2003

Hernan Crespo Inter Milan — Chelsea
£16.8m 2003

Claude Makelele Real Madrid — Chelsea
£16.6m 2003

All transfer figures are as reported in the media.

— RUSH ON ITALY —

'I couldn't settle in Italy... It was like living in a foreign country.'

Wales striker Ian Rush on his unhappy spell with Italian giants Juventus in 1987–88.

— FOOTBALL ON FILM —

Given its unrivalled international appeal, it should really come as no surprise that football – its players, teams, matches and so forth – has been the subject of numerous feature films since the first known big-screen soccer pic, *Harry The Footballer*, a black and white silent film made in 1911. (*The Winning Goal*, also made in Britain, followed in 1920.) Football is difficult both to stage and cut, so it follows that the number of sincerely dreadful football films far outweighs the gems. Here's a brief guide, with one star denoting the worst of the bunch and five stars highlighting the best.

The Goalie's Anxiety At The Penalty Kick (1971) A German film (directed by Wim Wenders) that proves to be an unexpectedly gripping psychological thriller. ★★★

Yesterday's Hero (1979) Features Ian McShane as the star striker for Leicester Forest on a predictable booze-and-birds bandwagon. John Motson commentates. ★

Escape To Victory (1981) Stars Michael Caine and Max Von Sydow, with Sylvester Stallone in goal. Pele, Bobby Moore and Ossie Ardiles feature along with a multitude of Ipswich players. Stuttering and stereotypical. ★★

Gregory's Girl (1981) The curiously appealing John Gordon Sinclair finds first love on the soccer pitch – and it's a girl. Can the inept goalie win this ace player's heart? Sweet. ★★★★

Those Glory, Glory Days (1983) Stars Zoe Nathenson as the young Spurs fan infatuated with charismatic club captain Danny Blanchflower. Julie Welch, sports writer for *The Observer*, wrote this autobiographical screenplay. ★★★

— FOOTBALL ON FILM (CONT'D) —

Young Giants (1983) Stars Pele and John Huston. The Brazilian soccer legend is the hero who helps to save an orphanage from closure through staging a football match. Pele's silky skills could not save this nonentity. ★★

Arrivederci Millwall (1991) Stars Kevin O'Donohoe. Millwall fans set out to support England in the 1982 World Cup finals in Spain. ★★★

Goals For Girls (1992) US film with comedian Rodney Dangerfield as coach. ★★

An Evening With Gary Lineker (1994) Stars Paul Merton, Martin Clunes and co-author Arthur Smith. Super stage play transforms to a fair film. Alistair McGowan provides the voice of John Motson. ★★★

There's Only One Jimmy Grimble (2000) Stars Jane Lapotaire, Gina McKee and Lewis McKenzie. A bullied boy seeks a road to glory. Traditional tale falls wide of the mark. ★★

A Shot At Glory (2000) Robert Duvall stars as a Scottish football club manager and Michael Keaton as his American club chairman. ★★★

Mike Bassett, England Manager (2001) Stars Ricky Tomlinson. Genuinely funny film although widely panned, perhaps because the on-screen antics did not match up to those of Keegan and company in the same era. ★★★★

Mean Machine (2001) Prisoners orchestrate a football match against guards to engineer a break-out. Vinnie Jones is the con and David Hemmings the prison governor. Missable. ★

Bend It Like Beckham (2002) Football and friendship film with Parminder Nagra and Keira Knightley. This affectionate skit was a surprise but worthy hit. ★★★★★

— MASCOTS BY TYPE AND NAME —

Nobody really knows why but just about all football clubs have a mascot that parades around the ground prior to a match. Mascots are inevitably outsized and furry. They do the same job as cheerleaders in American football but are significantly less glamorous. Indeed, sometimes they are controversial. Swansea's 9' (2.74m) mascot, Cyril The Swan, has incurred the wrath of the FA on more than one occasion. In 1999 he was deemed to have brought the game into disrepute with a pitch invasion. Two years later the Swan was in deep water again after drop-kicking the head of Millwall's mascot Zampa The Lion into the crowd during a 0–0 draw at the Vetch Field. Before the incident Cyril and Zampa squared up to one another, to the amusement and bemusement of watching fans. Deepdale Duck, the mascot attached to Preston North End, once had to be dragged from the field by its wings after being given a red card by the referee. The FA favoured a code of conduct in which mascots would be banned from the pitch, banned from taunting other fans and banned from behaving in a vulgar fashion. Here's a list of mascots you might encounter during Premiership matches:

Arsenal – Gunnersaurus Rex The Dinosaur

Blackburn Rovers – Roar The Lion

Birmingham – Beau Brummie

Bolton – Lofty Lion

Charlton – Floyd and Harvey

Chelsea – Stamford Lion

Everton – Mr Toffee

Fulham – Terry Bytes

Leeds – Ellie The Elephant

Leicester – Filbert Fox

Manchester City – Moonchester

Manchester United – Fred The Red

Middlesbrough – Roary Lion

— MASCOTS BY TYPE AND NAME (CONT'D) —

Newcastle – Monty Magpie

Portsmouth – Nelson The Dog

Southampton – Super Saint

Tottenham Hotspur – Chirpy The Cockerel

Wolves – Wolfie and Wendy

Note the monotonous regularity with which lions appear. For the record, there are more lion mascots in the other divisions including Gresty The Lion at Crewe Alexandra, Kingsley The Lion at Reading, Roary at Macclesfield, Lennie at Shrewsbury, Sandy Lion at Southport and Yorkie The Lion at York City.

THE ONLY FIVE CLUBS TO HAVE WON THE FIRST DIVISION TITLE IN THE — SEASON IMMEDIATELY FOLLOWING PROMOTION —

Nottingham Forest (1977–78)
Ipswich Town (1961–62)
Tottenham Hotspur (1950–51)
Everton (1931–32)
Liverpool (1905–06)

Only one club has won the title in its first-ever season at the top – step forward Sir Alf Ramsey's Ipswich heroes of '62.

— (DON'T) SING WHEN YOU'RE WINNING —

We're not making this up. In January 2004 supporters of Eastbourne Borough FC arrived at Cambridge City's ground for a Dr Martens League clash. Imagine their surprise to be met by a senior steward and told they should (a) not bang drums and (b) not chant too loudly.

He then explained there was an old people's home next to the stadium and that the club (average attendance 400) had been 'walking on eggshells' after noise complaints to the city council.

Julian Smith, one of the Eastbourne faithful, said, 'I've followed football for years and never come across anything like this.' City chief executive Arthur Eastham confirmed to *The Daily Telegraph* that the club had been warned about noise levels by the council: 'Cambridge is not exactly a hot-bed of football, so sometimes we do have a few problems,' he said. Could have been a Kevin Keegan quote.

— FOOTBALL BOOKS —

There are literally hundreds of books about football clubs. If you support Exeter or Everton, Manchester United or Macclesfield, you will surely find that a proud history and points record has been published for you to enjoy. But what about some more general titles, to cover different aspects of the game. Here's a reading list for you to work your way through, when you have a bit of time on your hands. Then you can move on to the biographies…

They Used To Play On Grass by Terry Venables (1971)

Flat Back Four: The Tactical Game by Andy Gray (1999)

Football Grounds by Jake Welsh (2003)

BBC Football Year Book 2003–04 by Terry Pratt

Casuals – The Story Of Terrace Fashion by Phil Thornton (2003)

Marvellous, Isn't It? The Autobiography by Ron Manager (2003)

Eurotrashed – The Rise And Rise Of Europe's Football Hooligans by Dougie Brimson (2003)

Playing Away: The A–Z of Soccer Sex Scandals by Matthew Clark (2003)

Boots, Balls And Haircuts by Hunter Davies (2003)

PFA Footballers' Who's Who 2003–04 by Barry Hugman

— MOTTYBALLS —

- 'For those of you watching in black and white, Spurs are in the all-yellow strip.'

- 'The World Cup is a truly international event.'

- 'I think this could be our best victory over Germany since the war.'

- 'Northern Ireland were in white, which was quite appropriate because three inches of snow had to be cleared from the pitch before kick off.'

- 'The goals made such a difference to the way this game went.'

- 'That shot might not have been as good as it might have been.'

- 'The match has become quite unpredictable, but it still looks as though Arsenal will win the cup.'

- 'Not the first half you might have expected, even though the score might suggest that it was.'

- 'And Seaman, just like a falling oak, manages to change direction.'

- 'Nearly all the Brazilian supporters are wearing yellow shirts – it's a fabulous kaleidoscope of colour.'

- 'That's an old Ipswich move – O'Callaghan crossing for Mariner to drive over the bar.'

- 'Bruce has got the taste of Wembley in his nostrils.'

- 'So different from the scenes in 1872, at the Cup final none of us can remember.'

- 'There is still nothing on the proverbial scoreboard.'

- *'It looks like a one-man show here, although there are two men involved.'*

- *'It's Arsenal 0, Everton 1, and the longer it stays like that the more you've got to fancy Everton.'*

- *'And what a time to score. Twenty-two minutes gone.'*

- *'It's a football stadium in the truest sense of the word.'*

- *'Actually, none of the players are wearing earrings, Kjeldberg, with his contact lenses is the closest we can get.'*

— WORD FROM OUR SPONSORS —

Incredible when you think about it, but 30 years ago the FA and TV bosses were refusing to allow footage of teams wearing a sponsors' logo. Hats off, therefore, to Wolves legend Derek Dougan who, as chief executive of Southern League stalwarts Kettering Town in 1975–76, sent his players out in shirts bearing the name of sponsors Kettering Tyres. The FA got tough and demanded the logo be removed. With a superb body-swerve – and some nifty needlework – Dougan then got the logo changed to read 'Kettering T'. He claimed the 'T' stood for Town. The FA banned it again.

— TAKE A FLYER —

Supporters often bemoan the cost of travelling to games but perhaps we should all take a leaf from Andy Rolle's book. In early 2004 he and fellow London-based Liverpool fan Chris Dominic were quoted £204 by Virgin for two return rail tickets to Merseyside for Liverpool's game against Villa. A quick shop-around established that two return flights with Ryanair cost roughly half this – provided the lads didn't mind travelling via Brussels.

They didn't. They jumped on a Stansted flight at 7:30am, landed in Brussels at 8:30am, waited an hour to change planes and touched down in Liverpool at 11:45am, leaving plenty of time for chips and a pre-match pint. 'It was perfect,' said Andy, 'especially when we beat Villa 1–0. But it's the first time I've needed my passport to see Liverpool play at Anfield.'

— BANK ON BECKS —

Remember all those jokes about Becks being a bit thick? You know: 'If Alan Shearer's got a Cruciate, Victoria, we're having one. I'm bored with the Bentley.'

However, Becks certainly *isn't* thick if financial success is anything to go by. According to accounts published in January 2004, his company Footwork Productions, which handles non-playing income, made an impressive £8.7 million the previous year – a £5.2 million increase on 2002. David paid himself £5.5 million in wages plus £1.25 million in share dividends. Add in the £4 million contract from Manchester United and there seems to be more than enough to keep Victoria in hair extensions.

In fact, Posh and Becks (or Dosh and Becks as the papers call them) can expect to push their income up still further in the years ahead. At the time of writing, David is only 28 and his Real Madrid earnings are estimated to be £90,000 a week.

For the benefit of trivia purists, the biggest Becks sponsorships and endorsements in recent years include:

Tokyo Beauty Centre	£2.5 million
Rage Software	£1.5 million
Vodafone	£1 million
Brylcreem	£1 million
Police sunglasses	£1 million
Pepsi	£250,000

According to newspaper gossip in February 2004 sportswear manufacturers Adidas are also lining up an 'ambassador' contract which could earn him anything up to £100 million over his lifetime. Despite all this, he's languishing behind US basketball star Michael Jordan in the all-time Sports Megabucks Champions League. Jordan's wealth is estimated at £250 million.

Those who have a pop at David for being (a) too rich or (b) too successful should remember that he gives big chunks of his fortune away – like the £70,000 gifted to disabled children's charities Children Today and Action for Kids in 2004. Just thought we'd mention it. Because he usually doesn't!

— THAT'S RICH —

Becks's wealth may seem obscene to some but bear in mind there's rich, very rich and Roman Abramovich. The Russian who has kitted Chelsea out in a sharp suit with bottomless pockets has earned around £7.2 billion from his oil and aluminium business empire. This makes him the richest man in Britain, comfortably beating off the challenge of Han Rausing (packaging; £6.6 billion), the Duke of Westminster (land and property; £4.63 billion) and Lakshmi Mittal (steel; £3.1 billion).

If you stuck Abramovich's fortune in a building society at, say, a 4.25 per cent standard rate of interest, it would earn £838,000 per day. After a year, Abramovich would be able to afford to buy Chelsea 51 times over or around 28 David Beckhams. Not bad for a chap who began his entrepreneurial career selling rubber ducks and plastic toys from a market stall somewhere in Russia's bit of the Arctic Circle.

— GEORGE BEST, THE PLEASURE AND THE PAIN —

Despite possessing some of the most awesome skills ever seen on a football pitch, Best's name remains closely associated with booze and birds. He became one of the original soccer bad boys who attracted salacious and sensational headlines on a weekly basis.

Best was spotted by a United talent scout when he was just 15 and brought across the Irish Sea to trial at Old Trafford. Soon he abandoned his amateur status and, on 14 September 1963, he made his debut against West Bromwich Albion. On his second outing some three months later against Burnley he scored.

Best scored 28 goals in 41 matches in the 1967–68 season, helping United to finish runners-up in the League. That made him United's top scorer that season, a position he maintained for four more seasons. He won both the Footballer Of The Year and the European Player Of The Year trophies.

— GEORGE BEST... (CONT'D) —

In a spot of synchronicity George Best made 361 League appearances for Manchester United scoring 136 goals. He also holds the record for the most goals by a United player in a single match (not including World War II), scoring six against Northampton Town on 8 February 1970 in the fifth round of the FA Cup. United won the match 8–2.

Early on his performances were sufficient to convince Northern Ireland's selectors that he was a 'must' for the team sheet. In 37 appearances for Northern Ireland he scored nine goals (although some statisticians prefer to say ten and include one scored against England's Gordon Banks that was controversially disallowed).

These were the golden years, marred in the 1970s by off-pitch antics that affected his consistency on the field. An on-off relationship with United finally ended in 1974 when he failed to turn up for training. He was just 27 years old.

After leaving Old Trafford his clubs have included Dunstable Town (1974), Stockport County (1975), Cork Celtic (1975), Fulham (1976–77), Hibernian (1979–80), Bournemouth (1983) and Brisbane Lions of Australia (1983).

Best also played in the short-lived North American Soccer League for LA Aztecs (1976–78), Fort Lauderdale Strikers (1978–79) and San Jose Earthquakes (1980–81), and made numerous guest appearances for teams in friendly, charity and testimonial matches. He played his final international match for Northern Ireland at the age of 35.

Here is a potted version of his greatest years:

- **1946:** Born 22 May in Belfast
- **1963:** Makes debut for Man Utd
- **1964:** Makes Northern Ireland debut
- **1965:** United win the League Championship
- **1968:** Voted English and European Footballer Of The Year and helps United to European Cup victory
- **1970:** Sent off for Northern Ireland for throwing mud at ref
- **1972:** Walks out on United aged 26
- **1974:** Best's association with United finally ends

— RICKY ROCKS WEMBLEY —

Picture the scene. It's May 1981, the replay of the 100th FA Cup final. Spurs have just levelled at 2–2 through Garth Crooks and there's 15 minutes before the torture of extra time. Suddenly, Argentinian Ricky Villa – substituted during a lacklustre performance the previous Saturday – wins possession 6 yards (5.5m) outside the City penalty area. In the ten glorious seconds that follow he somehow manages to out-Roy *Roy Of The Rovers*.

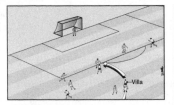

Villa wins possession

He advances into the penalty area and swerves wide past Caton's lunging tackle

Four City defenders surround him as he cuts back past a challenge from Ranson

Another magical body swerve takes him into space

City 'keeper Joe Corrigan sees the mounting panic in his defensive ranks and advances to close Villa's angle

Ricky slips the ball past another Caton tackle and, in the same delicate movement, steers it over Corrigan into the bottom-left corner

Most neutrals agree: it was the greatest individual goal in FA Cup final history.

— PLATT ON SVEN —

'When you speak to him you think what a nice, reasonable, intelligent, studious and plausible person he is... But there is a drive and a desire inside him that is not immediately apparent.'

David Platt on his former Sampdoria manager Sven-Goran Eriksson.

— LOAD OF TOSH —

Former Liverpool and Wales striker John Toshack is one of Britain's most durable soccer coaches. His career has spanned almost 30 years in what tabloid soccer writers like to call a 'roller coaster ride'. Here we map out the Trials of Toshack. Each event is marked by an OTM (Over The Moon) or an SAP (Sick As A Parrot).

1978	OTM	Tosh gets his first coach's job as player-manager with Fourth Division Swansea City.
1978	OTM	He steers them into the Third Division.
1979	OTM	And up to the Second.
1981	OTM	The Welsh maestro takes Swansea into the First Division for the first time ever. They top the table three times during that debut season and never drop out of the top six.
1983	SAP	Swansea are relegated and Tosh resigns.
1984	OTM	Tosh leaves to manage Sporting Lisbon.
1985–89	OTM	Moves to Real Sociedad, wins the Spanish Cup in 1987 and finishes second in '88.
1989–90	OTM	Becomes boss of Real Madrid. His team's league-winning tally of 107 goals remains a club record.
1990	SAP	Three defeats on the bounce and Real show him the door.

1991	**OTM**	It's back to Sociedad for another go.
1994	**SAP**	Wales come calling. Tosh takes the international job part-time but quits after just one game, a 3–1 defeat to Norway. Later the same year, Sociedad give him the elbow.
1995	**OTM**	A new challenge as coach to Deportivo La Coruna.
1997	**SAP**	Quits Deportivo.
1999	**OTM/ SAP**	*Hola!* Real Madrid. Toshack takes Guus Hiddink's old job. But then, same year, it's *hasta la vista* as Real apply the boot again.
2000	**OTM**	John gets a job with lowly French side St Etienne.
2001	**OTM**	Ten weeks later he's off! Real Sociedad just can't live without the man!
2002	**SAP**	Actually, they can. Sociedad sack him.
2002	**OTM**	John takes over at Serie B side Catania.
2003	**SAP**	Nope, it's not for him. Quits 12 weeks later.
2004	**OTM**	Tosh becomes new coach of Spanish outfit Murcia.

— LEBOEUF ON FAIR PLAY —

'English fair play is a myth. I have never seen so much violence on a pitch as in England. I don't want to indulge in English-bashing, but that's a fact.'

Former Chelsea defender Frank Leboeuf.

— DIGITAL DEBT —

The ITV Digital revolution, which had non-Premiership club chairmen salivating over promised riches, left main backer Carlton TV with an estimated £1.2 billion loss.

— ERIKSSON LOOKS FOR GROWTH —

'You are always looking for signs of the growth in confidence and composure; the belief that you can win any game if you set your mind to it.'

England coach Sven-Goran Eriksson comments on England's improving morale after his first year in charge and a famous victory over Germany.

— 1953 HUNGARIAN MASTERCLASS —

It was supposed to be a goodwill friendly in which England could show off and bang half-a-dozen goals past Hungary (wherever that was). In fact, nobody explained this to the Hungarians who promptly tore the English side apart with a dazzling display of skill, speed and inventiveness. The visitors won 6–3, with a hat-trick from centre-forward Hidegkuti, a 25-yarder (23m) from Bozsik and two beauties from the brilliant captain, Ferenc Puskas. It could easily have been ten.

The secret of the Hungarians' success lay in playing Hidegkuti deep, a strategy which left the English centre-half Johnston with no one to mark (see right). Sir Walter Winterbottom's 'WM' formation was no match for the visitors' fluid, flexible, 4–2–4 approach built around first-time passing and players who worked hardest when they were nowhere near the ball. An English side which took the field as Olympic Champions, unbeaten in three years and *never* beaten on home soil by foreign opposition, left humiliated and chastened. It was time for a re-think and the emergence of 4–4–2 as the staple English formation.

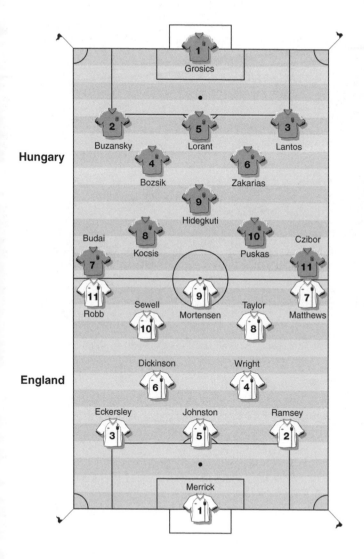

Hungary

Grosics 1

Buzansky 2   Lorant 5   Lantos 3

Bozsik 4   Zakarias 6

Hidegkuti 9

Budai 7   Kocsis 8   Puskas 10   Czibor 11

England

Robb 11   Sewell 10   Mortensen 9   Taylor 8   Matthews 7

Dickinson 6   Wright 4

Eckersley 3   Johnston 5   Ramsey 2

Merrick 1

— MANAGERS' SPECIALS —

A quotes 'shoot-out' among current and former managers illustrating the fine arts of punditry across six crucial categories.

PLAYER SKILLS

'Carlton Palmer can trap the ball further than I can kick it.'

– Ron Atkinson

'Despite his white boots, he has pace and aggression.'

– Kevin Keegan

'Even when they had Moore, Hurst and Peters, West Ham's average finish was about 17th. It just shows how crap the other eight of us were.'

– Harry Redknapp

'What can I say about Peter Shilton? Peter Shilton is Peter Shilton, and he has been Peter Shilton since the year dot.'

– Bobby Robson

'Michael Owen – he's got the legs of a salmon.'

– Craig Brown

'Robert Lee was able to do some running on his groin for the first time.'

– Glenn Hoddle

'Pires has got something about him: he can go both ways depending on who's facing him.'

– David Pleat

PLAYER BRICKBATS AND BOUQUETS

'I would not say David Ginola is the best left-winger in the Premiership, but there are none better.'

– Ron Atkinson

'Suker – first touch like a camel.'

– Ron Atkinson

'He actually looks a little twat, that Totti.'

– Ron Atkinson

'They compare Steve McManaman to Steve Heighway and he's nothing like him, but I can see why – it's because he's a bit different.'

– Kevin Keegan

'I don't think there is anybody bigger or smaller than Maradona.'

– Kevin Keegan

'Dani is so good-looking I don't know whether to play him or f*** him.'

– Harry Redknapp

'Hartson's got more previous than Jack The Ripper.'

– Harry Redknapp

THE NUMBERS GAME

'Now Manchester United are 2–1 down on aggregate, they are in a better position than when they started the game at 1–1.'

– Ron Atkinson

'We deserved to win this game after hammering them 0–0 in the first half.'

– Kevin Keegan

'Apart from their goals, Norway haven't scored.'

– Terry Venables

'When you are 4–0 up you should never lose 7–1.'

– Lawrie McMenemy

'You have got to miss them to score sometimes.'

– Dave Bassett

'They're two points behind us, so we're neck and neck.'

– Bobby Robson

'Well, we got nine and you can't score more than that.'

– Bobby Robson

— MANAGERS' SPECIALS (CONT'D) —

'Anything from 1–0 to 2–0 would be a nice result.'
– Bobby Robson

FOREIGN PARTS
(Note: Bobby Robson is the only real contender in this section, blowing away even Kevin Keegan with a truly tortuous understanding of the world atlas. Ron Greenwood's effort comes close though.)

'The Bulgarian players are tried and trusted. Well, I'm not sure they can be trusted.'
– Ron Atkinson

'Argentina won't be at Euro 2000 because they're from South America.'
– Kevin Keegan

'I came to Nantes two years ago and it's much the same today, except that it's totally different.'
– Kevin Keegan

'There'll be no siestas in Madrid tonight.'
– Kevin Keegan

'Where are we in relation to Europe? Not far from Dover.'
– Harry Redknapp

'Eighteen months ago they [Sweden] were arguably one of the best three teams in Europe, and that would include Germany, Holland, Russia and anybody else, if you like.'
– Bobby Robson

'We're taking 22 players to Italy, sorry, to Spain... where are we, Jim?'
– Bobby Robson

'Sarajevo isn't Hawaii.'
– Bobby Robson

'Playing with wingers is more effective against European sides like Brazil than English sides like Wales.'
– Ron Greenwood

MATCH ANALYSIS

'The 'keeper should have saved that one but he did.'
– Ron Atkinson

'Well Clive, it's all about the two M's. Movement and positioning.'
– Ron Atkinson

'If Glenn Hoddle said one word to his team at half time, it was concentration and focus.'
– Ron Atkinson

'You can't do better than go away from home and get a draw.'
– Kevin Keegan

'It was never part of our plans not to play well, it just happened that way.'
– Terry Venables

'They didn't change positions, they just moved the players around.'
– Terry Venables

'The Brazilians aren't as good as they used to be, or as they are now.'
– Kenny Dalglish

JUST BAFFLING

'I've seen some players with very big feet, and some with very small feet.'
– David Pleat

'I know what is around the corner – I just don't know where the corner is. But the onus is on us to perform and we must control the bandwagon.'
– Kevin Keegan

'Goalkeepers aren't born today until they're in their late 20s or 30s and sometimes not even then. Or so it would appear. To me anyway. Don't you think the same?'
– Kevin Keegan

— MANAGERS' SPECIALS (CONT'D) —

'I would have given my right arm to be a pianist.'

– Bobby Robson

'They can't be monks – we don't want them to be monks, we want them to be football players because a monk doesn't play football at this level.'

– Bobby Robson

'I played cricket for my local village. It was 40 overs per side, and the team that had the most runs won. It was that sort of football.'

– Bobby Robson

'It would be foolish to believe that automatic promotion is automatic in any way whatsoever.'

– Dave Bassett

'This is a real cat and carrot situation.'

– David Pleat

— PELE'S LITTLE LIST —

He may be the Beautiful Game's living legend but poor old Pele was spared no mercy by fans and players after compiling a list of the 100 greatest living footballers for FIFA's 2004 centenary year.

In the UK arguments raged long and hard. Pele found room for seven English players: Gordon Banks, David Beckham, Bobby Charlton, Kevin Keegan, Gary Lineker, Michael Owen and Alan Shearer. No place though for World Cup hat-trick hero Geoff Hurst. The Scots were happy with Kenny Dalglish, but how could the superb Denis Law miss out when he so rarely did in front of goal! As for the Welsh, Ryan Giggs failed to make the grade and FIFA confirmed that even if the late, great John Charles had survived for a few more days he wouldn't have got in. Only the Irish (George Best and Roy Keane) seemed appeased.

'It was very difficult choosing,' Pele explained later. 'Sometimes you have pain in your heart when you have to leave somebody out. Everyone has their own favourite 100 players and I just tried to make as few mistakes as possible.'

— VITAL STATISTICS OF THE PREMIERSHIP CLUBS —

ARSENAL
Stadium address: Arsenal Stadium, Highbury, London, N5 1BU
Capacity: 38,500
Ticket info hotline: 020 7704 4242

Club honours: League Champions 1930–31, 1932–33, 1933–34, 1934–35, 1937–38, 1947–48, 1952–53, 1970–71, 1988–89, 1990–91, 1997–98, 2001–02

Charity/Community Shield winners 1930, 1931, 1933, 1934, 1938, 1948, 1953, 1991, 1998, 1999, 2002

FA Cup winners 1930, 1936, 1950, 1971, 1979, 1993, 1998, 2002, 2003

League Cup winners 1987, 1993

European Cup Winners' Cup winners 1994

ASTON VILLA
Stadium address: Villa Park, Trinity Road, Birmingham, B6 6HE
Capacity: 42,584
Ticket info hotline: 0121 327 5353

Club honours: League Champions 1893–94, 1895–96, 1896–97, 1898–99, 1899–1900, 1909–10, 1980–81

Charity/Community Shield winners 1981

FA Cup winners 1887, 1895, 1897, 1905, 1913, 1920, 1957

League Cup winners 1961, 1975, 1977, 1994, 1996

European Cup winners 1982

BIRMINGHAM CITY
Stadium address: St Andrews, St Andrew's Street, Birmingham, B9 4NH
Capacity: 30,009
Ticket info hotline: 0121 772 0101

Club honours: League Cup winners 1963

BLACKBURN ROVERS
Stadium address: Ewood Park, Bolton Road, Blackburn, BB2 4JF
Capacity: 31,367
Ticket info hotline: 08701 123456

Club honours: League Champions 1911–12, 1913–14, 1994–95

Charity/Community Shield winners 1912

FA Cup winners 1884, 1885, 1886, 1890, 1891, 1928

League Cup winners 2002

BOLTON WANDERERS
Stadium address: Reebok Stadium, Burnden Way, Lostock, Bolton, BL6 6JW
Capacity: 27,879
Ticket info hotline: 08718 712932
Club honours: Charity/Community Shield winners 1958

FA Cup winners 1923, 1926, 1929, 1958

CHARLTON ATHLETIC
Stadium address: The Valley, Floyd Road, Charlton, London, SE7 8BL
Capacity: 26,500

Ticket info hotline: 020 8333 4010

Club honours: FA Cup winners 1947

CHELSEA
Stadium address: Stamford Bridge, London, SW6 1HS
Capacity: 42,420
Ticket info hotline: 020 7915 2951

Club honours: League Champions 1954–55

Charity/Community Shield winners 1955, 2000

FA Cup winners 1970, 1997, 2000

League Cup winners 1965, 1998

European Cup Winners' Cup winners 1971, 1998

EVERTON
Stadium address: Goodison Park, Liverpool, L4 4EL
Capacity: 40,260
Ticket info hotline: 0151 330 2200

Club honours: League Champions 1890–91, 1914–15, 1927–28, 1931–32, 1938–39, 1962–63, 1969–70, 1984–85, 1986–87

Charity/Community Shield winners 1928, 1932, 1963, 1970, 1984, 1985, 1986, 1987, 1995

FA Cup winners 1906, 1933, 1966, 1984, 1995

European Cup Winners' Cup winners 1985

FULHAM
Stadium address: Loftus Road, South Africa Road, London, W12 7PA
Capacity: 19,148
Ticket info hotline: 0870 442 1234

Club honours:

LEEDS UNITED
Stadium address: Elland Road, Leeds, LS11 0ES
Capacity: 40,204
Ticket info hotline: 09068 121 680

Club honours: League Champions 1968–69, 1973–74, 1991–92

Charity/Community Shield winners 1969, 1992

FA Cup winners 1972

League Cup winners 1968

LEICESTER CITY
Stadium address: The Walkers Stadium, Filbert Way, Leicester, LE2 7FL
Capacity: 32,500
Ticket info hotline: 0870 040 6000

Club honours: League Cup winners 1964, 1997, 2000

LIVERPOOL
Stadium address: Anfield, Anfield Road, Liverpool, L4 0TH
Capacity: 45,362

Ticket info hotline: 08704 444949

Club honours: League Champions 1900–01, 1905–06, 1921–22, 1922–23, 1946–47, 1963–64, 1965–66, 1972–73, 1975–76, 1976–77, 1978–79, 1979–80, 1981–82, 1982–83, 1983–84, 1985–86, 1987–88, 1989–90

Charity/Community Shield winners 1964, 1965, 1966, 1974, 1976, 1977, 1979, 1980, 1982, 1986, 1988, 1989, 1990, 2001

FA Cup winners 1965, 1974, 1986, 1989, 1992, 2001

League Cup winners 1981, 1982, 1983, 1984, 1995, 2001, 2003

European Cup winners 1977, 1978, 1981, 1984

UEFA Cup winners 1973, 1976, 2001

MANCHESTER CITY
Stadium address: The City Of Manchester Stadium, Sportcity, Manchester, M11 3FF
Capacity: 48,000
Ticket info hotline: 0870 4428000

Club honours: League Champions 1936–37, 1967–68

Charity/Community Shield winners 1937, 1968, 1972

FA Cup winners 1904, 1934, 1956, 1969

League Cup winners 1970, 1976

European Cup Winners' Cup winners 1970

MANCHESTER UNITED

Stadium address: Old Trafford, Sir Matt Busby Way, Manchester, M16 0RA
Capacity: 68,174
Ticket info hotline: 0870 7571968

Club honours: League Champions 1907–08, 1910–11, 1951–52, 1955–56, 1956–57, 1964–65, 1966–67, 1992–93, 1993–94, 1995–96, 1996–97, 1998–99, 1999–2000, 2000–01, 2002–03

Charity/Community Shield winners 1908, 1911, 1952, 1956, 1957, 1965, 1967, 1977, 1983, 1990, 1993, 1994, 1996, 1997, 2003

FA Cup winners 1909, 1948, 1963, 1977, 1983, 1985, 1990, 1994, 1996, 1999

League Cup winners 1992

European Cup winners 1968

Champions League winners 1999

European Cup Winners' Cup winners 1991

MIDDLESBROUGH
Stadium address: Riverside Stadium, Middlesbrough, Cleveland, TS3 6RS
Capacity: 35,049
Ticket info hotline: 01642 877 745

Club honours: League Cup winners 2004

NEWCASTLE UNITED
Stadium address: St James' Park, Newcastle-Upon-Tyne, NE1 4ST
Capacity: 52,218
Ticket info hotline: 0191 261 1571

Club honours: League Champions 1904–05, 1906–07, 1908–09, 1926–27

Charity/Community Shield winners 1909

FA Cup winners 1910, 1924, 1932, 1951, 1952, 1955

PORTSMOUTH
Stadium address: Fratton Park, Frogmore Road, Portsmouth, PO4 8RA
Capacity: 19,179
Ticket info hotline: 02392 618777

Club honours: League Champions 1948–49, 1949–50

Charity/Community Shield winners 1949

FA Cup winners 1939

SOUTHAMPTON
Stadium address: The Friends Provident St Mary's Stadium, Britannia Road,
Southampton, SO14 5FP
Capacity: 32,551
Ticket info hotline: 0870 2200 150

Club honours: FA Cup winners 1976

TOTTENHAM HOTSPUR

Stadium address: White Hart Lane, 748 High Road, Tottenham, London, N17 0AP
Capacity: 36,236
Ticket info hotline: 0870 420 5000

Club honours: League Champions 1950–51, 1960–61

Charity/Community Shield winners 1921, 1951, 1961, 1962, 1967, 1981, 1991

FA Cup winners 1901, 1921, 1961, 1962, 1967, 1981, 1982, 1991

League Cup winners 1971, 1973, 1999

European Cup Winners' Cup winners 1963

UEFA Cup winners 1972, 1984

WOLVERHAMPTON WANDERERS

Stadium address: Molineux Stadium, Waterloo Road, Wolverhampton, WV1 4QR
Capacity: 28,525
Ticket info hotline: 0870 4420123

Club honours: League Champions 1953–54, 1957–58, 1958–59
Charity/Community Shield winners 1959

FA Cup winners 1893, 1908, 1949, 1960

League Cup winners 1974, 1980
